Th Eden Valley Railway

by
Robert Western

THE OAKWOOD PRESS

© Oakwood Press and Robert Western 1997

British Library Cataloguing in Publication Data
A Record for this book is available from the British Library
ISBN 0 85361 486 5

Typeset by Oakwood Graphics.
Repro by Ford Graphics, Ringwood, Hants.
Printed by The Witney Press, Witney, Oxon.

In memory of

Admiral Russell Elliot

*without whom the Eden Valley Railway
would almost certainly never have been built.*

Kirkby Thore station.

Title Page: The coat of arms of the Eden Valley Railway in its final form, having been chosen from the six designs originally submitted.

Published by
The Oakwood Press
P.O. Box 122, Headington, Oxford OX3 8LU

Contents

Bridge 52 near Appleby East.   *Peter Walton*

The view down the main street at Appleby, from the castle. The Triumphal procession for the cutting of the first sod went this way, as did Admiral Russell Elliot to his last resting place in the graveyard of St Lawrence's Church, which can be seen at the bottom of the hill.
Author

Chapter One

That Other Eden

'Eden' may well evoke for many the picture of an idyllic paradise. The Vale of Eden, once in Westmorland, now in Cumbria, may not be quite what the imagination can conjure up, but it is, nevertheless, a pleasant, verdant and very fertile area of land. The Pennines border it to the south and east, and the Cumbrian Mountains form a border to the west.

The vale takes its name from the River Eden, which rises in the Pennines and flows through it in a north-westerly direction. In this section, it is usually a quiet, peaceful river, in sharp contrast to the fast-flowing ones which tumble through the hills around. Appleby, the old county town of Westmorland, is located in the middle of the vale, and in the area there are a number of residences which form important country seats, including the famous Lowther Castle, home of the Lonsdale family, and the well-known 'Yellow Earl'. Brougham Hall and Appleby Castle are two other notable residences.

This stretch of land must have been a paradise of sorts to the builders of the Settle and Carlisle Line, as they descended from the harshness and rigours of the Yorkshire Moors for the final section into Carlisle.

Bleak moors, with their hardy fell sheep, give way to pasture land where cattle graze, and the terrain here presents no major problems to the railway builder.

Yet the Midland, in its thrust to Scotland through the vale, was not the first railway to enter this green and pleasant land.

An inroad had already been made by builders who had to conquer an equally harsh terrain. They came from the east as they battled to bring their railway over Stainmore, in an attempt to link North East and North West. Their objective was to provide an alternative to the already existing Newcastle and Carlisle Railway.

It was eventually as a result of this railway over the wild tops of the Northern Pennines, that the idea for a railway to serve the Eden Valley came to fruition.

Chapter Two

Motives

If railways were the arteries of the industrial revolution, coal was the life-blood flowing along them. Yet, in addition, the wealth being created by developing natural resources, for example, in the production of iron and steel, required the facility to transport other minerals. It was often necessary to do this over long distances, to bring together the materials used in the manufacturing process. Landowners, eager to have a share in the developing market, were quick to grasp the need to promote railways, once it had been demonstrated beyond reasonable doubt that they could provide the sort of tractive power needed.

Whilst there may be dispute about where the cradle of the railways is located, the North-East of England has a strong claim as an area where they were nurtured. The Stockton and Darlington, one of the most famous of all railways, which had opened in 1825, began to look for ways of expansion.

Over in the North-West, in the Furness area of Lancashire, there was iron ore. The railway system was being developed to bring this, together with other commodities such as slate and copper, from a comparatively remote region to one of the main rail arteries, a line which would eventually become the West Coast Main Line. This would provide access to wider markets. Lord Burlington had been instrumental in the development in Furness; he had much to gain financially, and had the right contacts to enable him to be influential in promoting the Furness Railway, together with other companies which joined the Lancaster and Carlisle at Carnforth.

The proprietors of the Stockton and Darlington could see that a link across the Pennines, also to the West Coast Line and to the Furness District, would provide the facility for two-way traffic; pig-iron and iron ore eastwards, and coal and coke from the Durham Coalfield westwards.

The Newcastle-Carlisle Railway had opened in 1835, but this had not provided the facility which the markets in the South Durham area needed. As a result, moving coal and coke from that area proved expensive, given the monopoly of the Newcastle and Carlisle.

Eventually, to meet the needs of the South Durham Coalfield, and provide the opportunity to bring commodities such as pig-iron from the North-West, the South Durham and Lancashire Union Railway was promoted. It would not take an easy route, crossing, as it did, the Northern Pennines at Stainmore, ending at Tebay. The Bill for this railway received the Royal Assent in July 1857. However, before this came about, a series of discussions had taken place which determined the sequence of events leading up to the building of the Eden Valley Line.

Chapter Three

Ideas and Proposals
(1854-1858)

Captain (later, Admiral) Russell Elliot,* RN of Appleby was a man who undoubtedly felt very strongly about the importance which Appleby should maintain as the county town of Westmorland. He was, however, concerned: in his view, the town was rapidly losing its prestige. By the middle of the 1850s it had lost what in his opinion was a vital connection with the outside world, because the Mail Coach no longer visited Appleby, a result of the coming of the Lancaster and Carlisle Railway. Local trade was flagging and, even worse, there was talk that the assizes, normally held in Appleby, would be moved to Kendal. For Russell Elliot, that must have seemed like the last straw.

He had come to Appleby towards the end of a very successful naval career. He was born at Stobs Castle, Roxburgh, on 26th March, 1802, the son of Sir William Elliot, Bart, only three years before the historic Battle of Trafalgar. He entered the navy at the age of 12, two years after his father's death, and following his elder brother George. He went in as a volunteer and over the years had a distinguished career, travelling the world on board a variety of naval vessels.

Exactly when he arrived in Appleby is unknown. He had married in 1830, had four children and became a widower in 1843. However a report on the Appleby and Kirkby Stephen Agricultural Show in September 1860 mentions Mrs Russell Elliot of Appleby Castle, and a gravestone in St Lawrence's churchyard records that Henrietta Elliot, who died on 15th October, 1878, was the wife of Admiral Elliot. From this evidence it can be concluded that Russell Elliot remarried. He retired as a Rear Admiral in November 1867, some five years after the line opened and then, as was the rule, he rose in the retired list to full Admiral in 1869. His naval expertise was much sought after, we are told, by various governments, although he himself was a Liberal. Contemporary Press reports seem unsure whether he should be given the title Captain, Rear-Admiral or Admiral. All are used. For this account, he will be given the title 'Admiral'.

Here, then, was a man of considerable experience in taking hold of situations and being in control of them. No doubt a fiercely loyal man to any cause he embraced, he was, nevertheless, it seems, a man of considerable sensitivity, wisdom and insight. His unostentatious acts of charity were well known in Appleby. He was to become a leading figure in the formative years of the Eden Valley Railway.

Fortunately, Russell Elliot was not alone in his concern about the future of Appleby. Other worthies of Appleby and district, especially Sir Richard Tufton, Bart, of Appleby Castle, for whom he was acting steward, shared it as well.

To a small group of gentlemen there seemed to be a solution to the problem; a railway through Appleby. Railways were developing rapidly and seemed to be bringing prosperity to the places they served, and giving them the sort of importance Appleby deserved.

* See Author's Note (p.111)

Obviously, it is very difficult to read motives clearly, especially ulterior ones, into the comments made nearly 150 years ago, but it does seem that much of the drive to build what became the Eden Valley Railway came from a fierce loyalty to the county town of Appleby.

Later, the arguments for commerce were readily used: the transportation of coal, coke, iron ore, pig-iron and lime, together with the advantages of providing cheap fuel to the towns and villages of the Eden Valley. In spite of these, what seems to have driven the movement for a railway was a desire to keep Appleby on the map and at the centre of county affairs.

During the deliberations, one speaker at a public meeting made his views known: 'A railway is a *sine qua non* for the district; and if [we] do not get this [the EVR], we will get none at all and might advertise Appleby to let!'

In fact there had been at least three previous but abortive schemes that might have put Appleby on the railway map. The York and Carlisle Junction, the Northumberland and Lancashire Union and the Yorkshire and Glasgow Union, however, all became victims of the aftermath of the Railway Mania during the 1840s.

In 1854, the High Sheriff of Westmorland, William Wilkinson of Warcop, headed a group who considered a scheme to build a railway from either Hackthorpe or Clifton, on the Lancaster and Carlisle, via Appleby, Brough and over Stainmore to Barnard Castle. A public meeting was held in Appleby and the scheme received a lot of support. A committee was appointed, following this meeting, to follow the proposals through, but it would seem the war with Russia (The Crimean War) and its subsequent pressure on the money market resulted in the whole business falling into abeyance and nothing further happened. Further it was felt that it would be advisable to wait until the Darlington and Barnard Castle line had been completed and that possibly, by this time, the money markets might have eased. The Darlington and Barnard Castle opened in June 1856, at which point it seemed appropriate to reconsider the scheme discussed at Appleby.

Thomas Bouch, who had been provisionally appointed Engineer, and George Brown, who had been asked to represent the Appleby party, made approaches to the Darlington and Barnard Castle, but it seemed the plans, on the eastern side, had changed, the projected junction having become Tebay.

It is suggested this scheme had been kept secret, quite deliberately but, to quote a contemporary report, it 'oozed out'. Mr Fawcett, also of the Appleby group, working with Brown, met the Directors of the Darlington and Barnard Castle Company, personally, only to find that one group denied the allegation whilst another admitted it.

The Appleby group felt they could no longer trust the other side, and so they decided to proceed quite separately with the building of a line from Hackthorpe to Richmond instead of to Barnard Castle, and to let the Barnard Castle group get on with their own plans, if they so decided.

Russell Elliot was involved in these discussions, and clearly was uneasy about the way the situation was developing. Further, the suggestion from the Appleby group to promote a line to Richmond seemed to alarm the other party, known by now as the Durham or East County Men, and more discussions took place. Some progress was made in an attempt to unite the parties. The Durham men agreed to support the Appleby Plan provided that, if the proposed line was constructed, a branch was made from some point on Stainmore to Tebay.

Again, the Appleby group rejected this proposal, and so the Durham group said they would build such a branch themselves and at their own risk. The Appleby men rejected this proposal as well. No doubt they feared that a line to Tebay would provide a more direct route to the Lancaster and Carlisle and the West Cumberland coast, so downgrading the section through Appleby to Clifton.

It is during these deliberations that reference is made to 'The Westmoreland Railway'. This title seems to have been used for the Appleby Railway although, at first, it is not clear whether the words are intended to be an official title or are simply used to describe the scheme to provide a railway through Westmorland. Eventually it became the former.

One of the earliest references is in a poster dated 15th September, 1856. This announced that a meeting would take place in Appleby Town Hall:

Westmoreland Railway
The Provisional Committee are requested to attend a meeting to be holden at the Town Hall Appleby on Saturday, September 20, 1856, at 2 o'clock precisely, for the purpose of appointing the Provisional Directors.

> Edmund A Fawcett,
> Hon. Sec.
> Appleby, 15th September 1856.

This poster is followed only two days later by a quite extraordinary one, in which feelings seem to be running very high. A statement had appeared in *The Times* newspaper, no doubt intended to cause mischief and undermine any coming together of the two groups. The poster read as follows:

Westmorland Railway
'Barnard Castle Extension. The Directors of the Darlington and Barnard Castle Railway and the Directors of the Stockton and Darlington propose to apply to Parliament next session to extend the former line to join the Lancaster and Carlisle at Tebay. Lord Lonsdale and other Landlords in the West, it is understood, are favourable to the proposed line which, if carried out, will afford facilities for the supply of Durham Coal to the districts of Westmorland - *Times*'.

The above Paragraph is a gross Fabrication. The Earl of Lonsdale writes to me (on the 15th Instant) 'that he has received no communication whatsoever from the Proprietors of Railroads on the Eastern side of the County and further he is confident that he never gave an assent to that project'.

The truth is, that the
> Earl of Lonsdale
> Sir Richd Tufton, Bart,
> Lord Brougham

and all the Principal LANDED PROPRIETORS in the district through which the APPLEBY RAILWAY is intended to pass, are not only agreeable but heartily wish well and good speed to it.

This statement is published in order to prevent the Public being deceived by such ERRONEOUS PUBLICATIONS.

Lord Brougham was seen as the most important supporter the scheme could have. Fortunately he felt the railway to be vital for the Eden Valley and agreed to cut the first sod.

On Eagles' wings such false rumours fly
Whilst TRUTH can hardly breath - ere yet it die.

EDMUND A. FAWCETT,
Hon, Secretary.
Appleby, 17 Sept 1856.

Strong stuff. Little wonder that there were further disagreements.
The meeting at Appleby Town Hall clearly reflected the impact of this development. William Wilkinson took the chair. Provisional Directors were appointed: Hon. Col Lowther MP, Captain Russell Elliot [sic], William Wilkinson, William Crackanthorpe, Robert Addison, John Hill, Richard Tinkler and (another) Robert Addison.

William Crackanthorpe took the opportunity (we are told 'amidst loud cheers') fervently to pledge his support for the projected scheme, and urged conciliation with other parties involved.

Russell Elliot also spoke. He was keen to point out his concern that the district should have a railway to ensure its future prosperity. He expressed regret that there were plans for the Barnard Castle line to go to Tebay because he felt that was not in the best interests of Appleby.

Following the public meeting, the Provisional Directors present held another, in private, and then met the Secretary of the Barnard Castle and Darlington Railway at the King's Head Hotel. The East County men had asked the Secretary to convey their decision to abandon the line to Tebay, and hoped to have a joint meeting in Brough on the following Friday with a view to reverting to the plans of two years previously, to take the line to Barnard Castle (not Richmond).

Shortly afterwards, an anonymous tract appeared. This was dated 30th September, 1856 and was signed 'An Inhabitant of Appleby'. In part, it reads as follows:

To the inhabitants of Westmoreland

Having been informed that gentlemen representing important interests are willing to co-operate in the formation of a railway from Barnard Castle by Kirkby Stephen, Musgrave, Brough, Warcop and Appleby to Clifton, with a short branch to Tebay, I venture with great deference to state that in my judgement such a railway if made will prove of the greatest value.

[The writer then goes on to give reasons. In essence:]

1. It will open the resources of the county and will make Westmoreland the great highway between the Northern Ocean and the Irish Sea . . . and between the Coal and Iron producing districts . . . of the kingdom.

2. Without undervaluing the projected Hilbeck line of 1854 I think the proposed line would be better for the county. On the Hilbeck line there would probably be only one station between Stainmore and Appleby and the position of it would prove difficult for access by the people of Brough, Kirkby Stephen, Musgrave, Warcop and adjacent places . . . The new line would pass on low ground . . . More people would find a use for it.

3. By its connections with Tebay would be given to Northern and Eastern parts of the kingdom access to the South.

[The writer has some reservations at this point, and in this connection, with the Clifton Line].

4. It would cheapen the price of coal.
5. The proposed valley line is a fair and honest railway the population of Westmoreland . . . It provides great commercial interest for East and West. It is therefore not a railway for one or two men, but the county - for, in fact, the kingdom.

[The document concludes with the words:]

I would humbly suggest that it would be wise to unite our energies and capital to carry it, thus accepting the benefits within our reach rather than pursuing shadows and cherishing visionary schemes of immense length, magnitude and cost which no-one will ever find the capital to carry out.

It is not easy to see why the writer chose not to disclose his identity. The document is not, on the face of it, contentious, but in some ways has a conciliatory tone. It was almost certainly produced in large quantities and the costly nature of the exercise suggests someone well-to-do; of course, it may have been produced by a group of people.

In spite of efforts at reconciliation, it seemed impossible to get agreement. The Tebay route again became an issue. Russell Elliot rather despondently wrote a letter on 10th November to Thomas Bouch, expressing his feelings:

I took care to lay your letter addressed to myself and one to Mr Wilkinson, late chairman of our Provisional Directors, before the committee.

I have nothing to say from the committee - as an individual I cannot conceal my chagrin at the course matters have taken and this more especially as I received with favour the propositions of the East County Gentlemen especially any scheme that gave a railway to this district and I feel much the position it has left one in viz. no choice to Sir Richard Tufton but to oppose energetically the Tebay line unless in acceding to it there is a moral and legal certainty of a line at the same time to Clifton.

It is apparent, however, that Admiral Elliot, together with some of his colleagues, felt that Mr Wilkinson had possibly taken too hard a line in the discussions, and that the proposals made by the other side were worthy of further consideration. At this point, the Appleby men were themselves divided, and so the Appleby committee 'melted away' (to use the words of Admiral Elliot). The Durham group was no doubt disappointed at the outcome, and now there was again a threat of opposition to their scheme.

The letter to Bouch indicates that Admiral Elliot was still very keen that Appleby should get railway communication. He then worked closely with Sir Richard Tufton, and once again approached the Durham group with a view this time to securing the insertion of clauses to enable either the link-up or part-use of the proposed Tebay line.

The previous abortive encounters, with the differences, seem fortunately not to have unduly upset the Durham party, whose members were still well disposed to an Appleby Railway. The outcome was that the Durham group agreed to the insertion of the clauses.

As things turned out, the proposed clauses were not acceptable, as far as Parliamentary procedures were concerned, and so could not be included. To offset this, an agreement was reached at a local level, in such a way that Admiral Elliot and Sir Richard Tufton withdrew opposition to the Bill. This step in turn opened the way to an Eden Valley Bill going forward.

The tables were now, of course, in effect turned. This time, the Appleby group had to approach the Durham party to support the making of a branch line. On this occasion, there was agreement.

During this time, in the initial stages of discussion, Admiral Elliot had also approached the Lancaster and Carlisle Railway Company (L&C) and was invited to a Board meeting. He explained the objectives of the Appleby group to build a railway from Clifton to Kirkby Stephen, but the L&C Board felt it could not offer to help the Appleby group, and pointed out that, whilst a junction at their Clifton station was acceptable, one at Clifton village would not be.

Admiral Elliot had further enquired whether the L&C Board would have any objection to the Appleby group approaching the Stockton & Darlington (S&D). He was informed there would be no objection, and when the S&D were approached, they, understandably, proved more than willing to support, agreeing to guarantee £25,000 of shares and to work the line.

Following these various discussions, the members of the Appleby group felt confident that their plans could succeed, and so they took a significant step: a company was formed and a Prospectus was planned.

A drawing of Admiral Russell Elliot, taken from a contemporary political cartoon.
Courtesy Brigadier J. Heelis

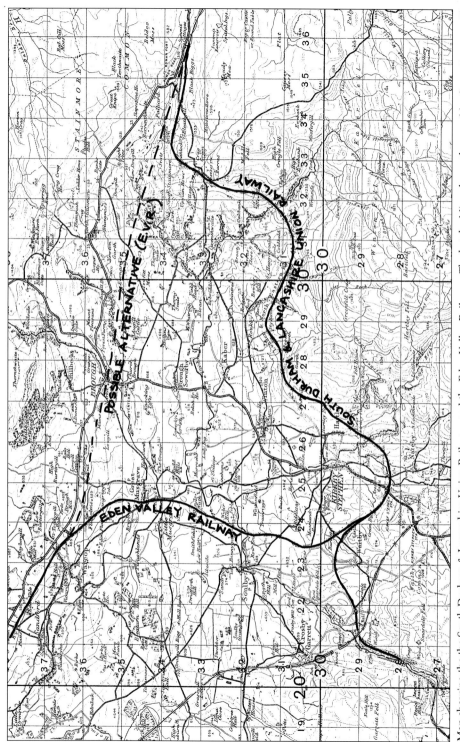

Map showing the the South Durham & Lancashire Union Railway and the Eden Valley Railway. The hatched line shows the possible alternative route if the Maiden Castle Junction had been accepted.

Chapter Four

The Prospectus

The draft Prospectus drawn up (for the Westmorland Railway) is dated 24th October, 1857. It is written in hand but has no details of names. Gaps are left for the insertion of these later.

A second draft has a number of details pencilled in. The words 'Westmorland Railway' have been crossed out and pencilled in over the top is the title 'Eden Valley Railway' (EVR).

The final form of the Prospectus appeared at the beginning of December 1857. It stated that the capital to be raised would be £135,000, and this would be realised through 5,400 shares at £25 each. The length of the line would be 22 miles.

Thirty-seven provisional Directors are named. At the head of the list is the Right Honourable Lord Brougham of Brougham Hall, whose support was considered to be of vital importance. He was very much a Westmorland man, Brougham Hall being near Penrith. His influence in a number of quarters was considerable.

Getting Lord Brougham's name on the list was something of a personal triumph for Russell Elliot because his lordship, whilst not being opposed to railways, seems to have had a dislike of them. His comments at the ceremony when the first sod was cut indicate this and yet Russell Elliot clearly saw his lordship's support for the scheme as being essential for its success. He approached Lord Brougham, who felt the provision of a railway in the Eden Valley to be worthy of support and in a letter of 10th November, 1857, sent to George Brown, Russell Elliot was able to write:

> I have just heard from Lord Brougham that although he has vowed never to hold any shares in any railway, he feels so much interest in the success of the Eden Valley scheme that he authorises his name to be placed on the List of Provisional Directors, that he might give it any other support in his power.

Other names worthy of mention are Sir Richard Tufton, Bart, of Appleby Castle, Admiral Russell Elliot of Appleby Castle and William Crackanthorpe of Newbiggin Hall. Edward Pease, MP for Darlington, is also on the list.

Russell Elliot had written to the Secretary, Brown, on 27th October, 1857, pointing out that the Lord Brougham had urged him 'to solicit the favour of Mr Pease and his friends, permitting their names to appear on the Provisional Committee' (and also to include Lord Bective).

In fact, Pease had arranged for the Parliamentary side of the business, and Lord Bective agreed to guide the EVR Bill through Parliament. The unexpected demise of Edward Pease, before the railway was started, was a matter of some lament. There are three clergymen listed, Reverend Joseph Milner of Appleby, The Reverend W.S. Preston of Warcop Hall, and The Reverend John Richardson, also of Appleby.

The treasurers were to be Messrs Mewburn, Hutchinson and Mewburn, of Darlington.

Thomas Bouch, approached a number of years before, became the Engineer. His name almost certainly calls to mind, for many people, the Tay Bridge, evoking nightmarish pictures of a locomotive and coaches plunging into the icy-cold Tay on a dark winter evening, with the loss of all on board.

However, the Eden Valley project was proposed long before the Tay Bridge disaster, at a time when Thomas Bouch enjoyed a good reputation.

Born in Thursby on 22nd February, 1822, Bouch was a Cumberland man, educated at the village school and then in Carlisle. He eventually found work on the Lancaster and Carlisle Railway, working under Larmer, the Resident Engineer, and later moved on to the Stockton and Darlington.

He became Engineer and Manager of the Edinburgh and Northern, and was involved in the building of the Darlington and Barnard Castle Line, which opened in 1856. He then became involved with the Kinross-shire and Leslie, and was already involved by this time in the South Durham and Lancashire Union Railway (SD&LUR) over Stainmore to Tebay, which gave rise to the Eden Valley Railway.

The South Durham and Lancashire Union is reckoned to be Bouch's finest work. One of its most famous structures was the impressive Belah viaduct. Like a number of his viaducts (for example Deepdale and Bilston Burn) it had an open lattice structure. He seemed to favour this design for its simplicity and, possibly, his experience of the high winds and driving rain in his home area led him to the conclusion that this type of structure offered least resistance to the elements, although there were drivers who refused to take trains over the Belah viaduct up to the day it closed, because of what had happened at the Firth of Tay.

Thomas Bouch, then, was the obvious choice for the Eden Valley Line. It was a natural development from his SD&LUR, and besides that he was renowned for his inexpensive schemes!

Later, he was to plan the Cockermouth, Keswick and Penrith Railway, which was to have important consequences for the prosperity of the Eden Valley Line.

In the Prospectus, it was made clear that the Eden Valley Railway would complete an important link between the railways of the North-East and those in the West. The mineral interests of South Durham and Westmorland and Cumberland would be well served.

Further, the EVR would form the shortest route from York, Cleveland and South Durham to Carlisle, Glasgow and South-West Scotland, cutting 20 miles off existing routes.

There would be other advantages of a more local nature. Penrith, Appleby, Brough and Kirkby Stephen would be linked, together with intervening villages, such as Kirkby Thore, Temple Sowerby and Warcop. This would provide them with a link into the outside world. The observation was also made that the important Westmorland and Cumberland fairs would be served.

There was, of course, the other reason, not mentioned in the Prospectus, namely the aim to keep Appleby as an important centre within the county. As was ever the case with the early railways, the over-riding argument was of a commercial nature. The coal and coke of the Durham Coalfield would be taken west, and the pig-iron and iron ore from Cumberland would find a market in South Durham.

It was pointed out that the line proposed would be comparatively simple to build. There were no severe gradients, and the cost was reckoned at about £6,100 per mile. It was anticipated that the line would be built quite quickly; in fact, in time to receive traffic at the same time that the SD&LUR was completed. It was estimated that a mileage receipt of £15 per week would pay a dividend of 6 per cent per annum, after allowing 50 per cent for working expenses.

The promoters, as we have seen, felt there would be advantages in working their line in close conjunction with the SD&LUR, and in view of this, and in order to save money, they decided, in their Bill, to empower adjoining companies to work the line, thereby eliminating the need to purchase engines and rolling stock. Already, as the Prospectus was being prepared, suitable terms were being negotiated with the Stockton and Darlington Railway.

The line proposed was not in competition with any other lines in the immediate vicinity. The whole scheme, including the SD&LUR, was an alternative to the Newcastle and Carlisle, but the latter was mainly of service to North Durham, and so there were no fears that the Bill would meet opposition from other companies. As a result, the promoters were confident in inviting applications for shares. In fact, in spite of its amicable disposition, the L&C was rather nervous about the scheme. They were anxious to ensure that it was only a local line, and would not have the potential to form part of a route to Scotland. Perhaps they felt that the deliberations involving what became the Ingleton branch, with its potential as a Scottish route and a possible threat, was quite enough, without similar threats from the Eden Valley Line.

At a meeting on 13th November, 1857, two possible routes were considered, one either side of the Eden. There was also some disagreement within the Appleby group about the route of the line, eastwards beyond Warcop, but an uneasy agreement was eventually reached. The line agreed upon was, in effect, a single track railway. Working from east to west (which seems to be the natural way to think of it, although the Act describes it as 'from the Lancaster and Carlisle . . . to the SD&LUR'), it started in the complex of tracks forming Kirkby Stephen station.

It left the station to the north of the main SD&LUR, running parallel to it for a short distance, before turning north into the Eden Valley. It crossed Scandal Beck and then the River Eden at Great Musgrave, where there was one of the two large viaducts on the line. This viaduct was 221 ft long and had three spans of iron. It was some 20 feet above the river at its highest point. Great Musgrave had a station with a small adjoining siding.

There was some dispute about whether or not Musgrave justified a station, and the debate prompted Mr G.H. Bailey of Brough to write to the Secretary of the company. The letter is dated 27th November, 1858. Mr Bailey writes:

Allow me to lay before you my thoughts which are identical with those of the whole of the inhabitants of Brough, indeed I may say the Parish and also that of the Parish of Musgrave . . .

The letter goes on to ask that a station should be sited 'as near as possible to the New Inn at Great Musgrave'. Mr Bailey lists reasons:

1.   The population of Brough and Musgrave is greater than either Warcop or Soulby - thus Musgrave is preferred. (The count of 1851 gave the population of Brough as 773 and the Parish as 1,536. The Parish of Great Musgrave numbered 238. In comparison, the whole of Warcop totalled 740 and Soulby 309.)

2.   Much more traffic would be likely to come from Brough and Musgrave because there are 18 shopkeepers who need merchandise coming in from Manchester, Liverpool, Carlisle, Penrith and Kendal. There are 3 corn mills 'constantly kept grinding corn', chiefly from Appleby and Penrith. '4 Bacon Factors' [sic]. Dealers in manures, 4 carriers.
     In addition, there is lead ore to be moved, and haematite which is yet to be worked.

3.   Musgrave is the most central place for a station.

4.   Musgrave is the largest place nearest Brough through which the railway passes.

5.   If mail bags are ever carried, Musgrave is the nearest place from which to receive mail from Brough.

Mr Bailey then lists his objections to any proposals to site a station at Soulby:

1.   Only a few would benefit and traffic would be lost.
2.   It is near Kirkby Stephen, which will have its own station.

He concludes by pointing out that 'as far as stone is concerned, most would have to be got from above Brough for the bridge over the Eden and for the station houses.' Finally,

> If the reasons I have given are not sufficient for the accommodation of Brough I cannot but think there has been a predetermination that Brough should be left without any railway accommodation.
> Let me know your decision for it is the last ray of hope that is left to it.

Whether the 'arm-twisting' in the penultimate paragraph, or the emotive plea in the last, had any influence, we shall never know; Musgrave, nevertheless, got a station!

After this, the line turned north-westwards, passing just to the north of the market town of Warcop. The facilities at Warcop were considerable. There were cattle pens, with amenities for the Horse Fair held at nearby Brough, a coal yard and goods sheds. Later, limestone was brought to the line for loading and a special point was provided for this. Later still, to meet the needs of the Army Training Area there were the means to handle ammunition and a special unloading point for armoured vehicles, such as tanks.

The signal box was originally located to the south of the track (*see map*) but later this box was replaced by one built on the east end of the station platform. The station building was also considerably rebuilt and made larger, with a second storey.

The line continued north-westwards to Appleby. Just before the old county town, it crossed (and still does) the Coupland Beck on a stone viaduct 200 feet long, which had five arches. There was a station at Appleby, and the next after that was at Kirkby Thore.

There was a debate about the siting of the station at Kirkby Thore. John Nicholson wrote to the Secretary on 25th November, 1858, saying he urged the company to site the station as near to the village as possible - or 'on the Kirkby Thore side of where the railway crosses the turn-pike road near Kirkby Thore Bridge End'.

Following this, the line turned westwards, passing well to the south of Temple Sowerby, which nevertheless had a station. Beyond Temple Sowerby, it crossed the Eden again, over the impressive Skygarth viaduct. This viaduct was skew to the line of the river, which resulted in it being longer than the width of the river might have dictated. It was 440 ft long, in consequence, and had four iron spans. It was 35 ft above the river at its highest point. After this, the line passed to the north of Cliburn, which was served by a small station some distance from the village.

After Cliburn, the line ran alongside woodland, eventually passing Weatheriggs Pottery, served by a siding. The line then turned south to a junction with the Lancaster and Carlisle, just south of Clifton. As it turned out, this south-facing junction was to meet the requirements of the L&C, as discussed by the Board with Admiral Elliot. Traffic from the line would have to go south, so that the L&C would achieve its objective of ensuring that the EVR was a local line, offering no threat as a Scottish route. The next significant place south on the L&C is Tebay, where the SD&LUR would have its own junction. As things turned out, this south junction was, in fact, short-lived. The coming of the Cockermouth, Keswick and Penrith Railway promoted the building of a north-facing junction, as will become apparent later.

Once the promoters had put their plans forward, it was agreed that a public meeting, intended to fire enthusiasm in the locality and so gain public support, would be desirable. Such a meeting was held in the Shire Hall in Appleby on Saturday 20th December, 1857.

The meeting, called by the Mayor, was to comply with a requisition 'to consider and determine upon the measures which it might be desirable should be taken for giving support to the line of railway projected through that part of the county, called the Eden Valley Railway.'

Speakers included Admiral Elliot, Mr Crackanthorpe, the Revd Joseph Milner and Mr Brown, the Secretary. The whole tone of the meeting was very positive, and those who attended, through their cheers and applause, indicated a keen support of the project.

The speakers emphasised, in particular, the ways in which the locality would benefit, the most obvious, in their opinion, being that fuel would be cheaper. A lot of play was made of the notion that people who were warm and comfortable were contented people, and the cheaper fuel would help this.

Land owners were urged not to listen to opponents who had tried to discourage them from buying shares. They were also told there was no truth in the information put about by some 'mischievous' persons that signing the Parliamentary notice 'assentient' would result in the owner having to accept whatever the company's surveyors might offer for the land to be purchased (inferring the land would therefore be undervalued). Those signing

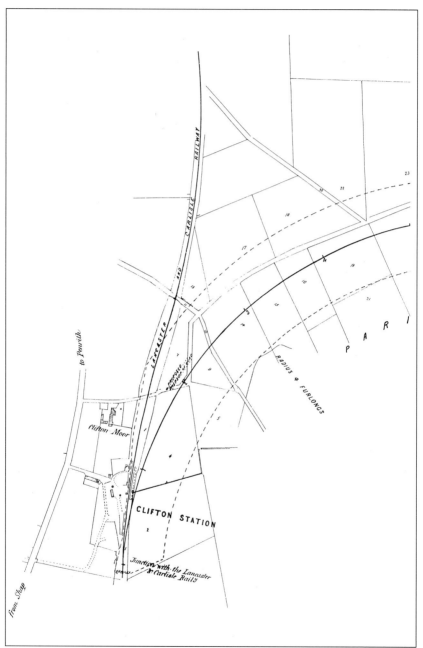

The original south-facing junction at Clifton station (Lancaster & Carlisle Railway) from the deposited plans for the EVR. *Cumbria Record Office*

'assentient', the meeting was told, would be dealt with generously. This point was to some extent emphasised by the (intentionally) humorous suggestion that signing 'dissentient' would lead to the owner's claim being resisted.

There appears to have been some chicanery involving the signing of agreements and later, in a letter written on 28th December, 1857, Russell Elliot had occasion to mention possible forged signatures amongst those whom he knew to be 'assentients' but who appeared as 'dissentients' in the lists.

As mentioned previously, there had been some disagreement about the route of the line and at the meeting there was a further attempt to appease the group which had wanted a route which would go to Maiden Castle in order to give better benefit to Brough.

Maiden Castle is the site of a Roman Fort, situated on the west side of Stainmore adjacent to the Maiden Way, a Roman Road. At this place the SD&LUR turns south before making a wide arc round to Kirkby Stephen.

Taking the Eden Valley Line from Warcop in a generally easterly direction would have brought it to a junction with the SD&LUR at Maiden Castle in such a way that the line would have passed close to Brough. The route as constructed deprived Brough of a valuable railway facility, and, according to contemporary accounts, Brough Fair, in particular, suffered as a result.

However, Kirkby Stephen provided a more satisfactory point of junction; Maiden Castle would have been too remote to be practical.

The speakers were eloquent and convincing, and it seems that those present were indeed convinced and, judging by their response, supported the scheme wholeheartedly.

In an optimistic frame of mind, the promoters put forward their Bill, which went through the Parliamentary procedure quite smoothly. The L&C raised no objections, given the plan for a south-facing junction at the westerly end of the line. The Act (Vict. Reg. 21, Cap. xiv) was incorporated on 21st May, 1858.

Following the success of the passage of the Bill through Parliament and the passing of the Act, a general meeting of the shareholders was called, and this took place at the King's Head Hotel in Appleby on Saturday 12th June, 1858. Admiral Elliot was in the chair, and the gathered company included William Brougham, John Crosby, William Crackanthorpe and William Hopes.

Admiral Elliot savoured the event as a moment of triumph, congratulating those present on the fact that they had become the proprietors of the Eden Valley Railway. He was in a confident mood, and felt that the prospects were good.

Thomas Bouch was unable to be present, as he was giving evidence before a Parliamentary Committee on the Hawick and Carlisle Railway Bill.

Mr Brown, the Secretary, read the report of the Directors. Again there was cause for congratulations. The requisite powers for the construction of the railway had not met with opposition in either House. Further, satisfaction was recorded on resolutions of approval of the Bill passed in the previous April, involving the railways with which the EVR was connected: the S&D, SD&LUR and the L&C.

Following the formalisation of certain financial aspects, it was announced that Thomas Bouch had been asked to mature his survey so that tenders could be invited. In addition, once more detailed information was available, land owners would be approached regarding the sale of land. By this time, the centre line of the railway had already been staked out.

With the passing of the Act, the existing Directors all resigned, but a proposal to re-elect the group was carried unanimously, and so the Board elected consisted of Admiral Russell Elliot, Sir Richard Tufton, Bart, Edward Pease MP, William Crackanthorpe, William Hopes, John Crosby, Isaac Wilson, Robert Addison, William Brougham, James Atkinson, John Whitwell and W.R.J. Hopkins.

Following this, Thomas Bouch was formally appointed the Engineer, Mr Brown the Secretary and Thomas Macney and John Crosby, Junior, were appointed auditors. Thomas Macney was also the Secretary of the S&D.

In conclusion, Admiral Elliot pointed out that shares were still available, and he urged those present to find buyers.

Shortly after the meeting, Admiral Elliot was appointed Chairman and Mr William Hopes, Vice-Chairman.

The way was now clear to proceed with all haste. It was anticipated that the line would take only two years to build, a projection which proved to be too optimistic. However, spirits were high. Admiral Elliot must have felt a great sense of satisfaction that Appleby had been saved from oblivion!

At a half-yearly meeting of the SD&LUR on 3rd August, 1858, at the King's Head Inn, Barnard Castle, the Secretary noted with some satisfaction:

Since your last meeting, the Act for the Eden Valley Railway has received the Royal Assent, and the Directors of that railway hope to be able to open for traffic simultaneously with that of your own railway.

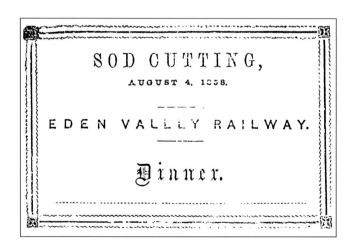

SOD CUTTING,

AUGUST 4, 1858.

EDEN VALLEY RAILWAY.

Dinner.

Chapter Five

Cutting the First Sod
(1858)

In euphoric mood, the Directors decided to make a big event out of cutting the first sod. Whilst the festivities which accompanied the opening of new railways were often very elaborate, and it seemed no expense was spared, with all those involved in the project, from the Directors to the navvies, being given an opportunity to celebrate and indulge themselves, the Directors of the Eden Valley Railway made this initial ceremony a major event. The number of people drawn into the festivities which resulted, ran into thousands.

In fact a small special committee consisting of three men, Messrs Thompson, Robinson and Mason, had been set up almost a year before, the first meeting being held on 7th August, 1857. The group considered suitable arrangements and one of the first requests directed to the finance committee was for the provision of a special wheelbarrow!

Almost a year later, when the date of the ceremony had been fixed for 4th August, printed letters were sent to those invited to attend. Russell Elliot's name (spelt 'Eliott', *see Author's Note p.111*) appears at the bottom. In addition, those invited to be guests at the dinner at 2.30 pm were sent special invitations printed in gold on white card.

Further, the committee produced a lengthy guest list and 116 of those invited indicated they would be present. A list of 15 toasts was printed and 14 banners and 16 flagpoles were ordered from Barnard Castle.

The location of the ceremony was in a field to the right of the Battlebarrow road between Appleby and Penrith, about half a mile from Appleby. An arena of sorts was built by fencing off a rectangular-shaped piece of ground, and seats were provided for the ladies, who, according to the accounts, were present in large numbers.

The site where the cutting actually took place by no means confined the celebrations. It was reported that nobody within living memory could recall the town of Appleby being so festively adorned. A number of triumphal arches were built, which were elaborately decorated, and many houses were decked with flags and banners. Five of the arches were especially fine, displaying crowns of flowers, evergreens and flags. Slogans such as 'Success to the Eden Valley Railway' and 'Long Live Sir Richard Tufton' were used, together with pictures showing an engine and carriages, the British Lion protecting the British Flag, and Admiral Elliot's naval flag.

The county surveyor, Mr George Robertson, was responsible for organising this magnificent and striking display. So impressive were these arches, that visitors from a wide area in the Eden Valley came to see them, and, on the day of the actual cutting, large numbers came into town. This was, not surprisingly, taken by some to indicate how much the coming of a railway was welcomed in the district; especially at Appleby.

Another attraction was that Lord Brougham had agreed to be the guest of honour and to cut the first sod. Shortly after 11 am, he was escorted from

Appleby Castle by the Directors of the line, principally in the company of Sir Richard Tufton.

A long procession formed up to accompany the group. This included, in order, a thousand children from Appleby and the surrounding parishes, a cavalry band, two hundred Oddfellows, the Dutton Band, over one hundred Foresters, and the Alston Band. Finally, the Appleby band preceded the main party.

The weather was fine, to begin with. A mahogany wheelbarrow with ornamental spade was made ready, but before the main business was started, Admiral Elliot, as Chairman, addressed the company at the field. He gave a stirring speech, which drew applause on several occasions. In a dramatic stance, he pointed out that 'the day has now arrived for which we have so anxiously looked; nay, the hour, the minute approaches when all our hopes, all our fears, all our assertions are to be consummated by the practical commencement of the Eden Valley Railway.' He recalled the difficulties they had faced, the problems they had overcome, and went on: 'Even this time last year, the only capital which we possessed was our hope and determination. Active resistance, passive apathy. Both have been faced and defeated.'

The crowd seemed impressed. There were words of high praise for Lord Brougham 'ever identified with Westmorland . . . who was about to serve his native county in a new capacity, that of a navvy.'

After this accolade (which was by no means the only one of the day), Lord Brougham shovelled several sods of earth into the ornamental barrow, wheeled them to the end of a plank, emptied them and brought the barrow back again.

Lord Brougham cutting the first sod of the Eden Valley Railway at Appleby as depicted in the *Illustrated Times*.   *British Library Newspaper Library, Colindale*

Having completed this task, he then took his turn in speaking to the crowd. He sang the praises of the scheme, saying that agriculture and trade would benefit from its completion. There were some political innuendos in the speech, but his main theme was to commend those who had brought the scheme to fruition.

After his lordship had finished, William Crackanthorpe, another Director, spoke. Once again, the praise and the congratulations flowed. He made some interesting observations about the position of Appleby and its importance. He recalled, for example, the days when the mail coach stopped to change horses, and Appleby was a considerable posting town. The mail coach had gone. The Lancaster and Carlisle Railway had put paid to that! Appleby had become something of a backwater, losing its communication with the outside world. This had been a matter for considerable concern, but with the coming of the railway, trade, in Mr Crackanthorpe's view, would recover, and the town's vitality would be restored. The poor would have fuel at a cheaper rate, and other advantages would follow.

The final speaker of the morning was the mayor of Kendal, Mr J.J. Wilson. He drew a great ovation from the crowd by insisting that the Eden Valley Railway would be the means of binding together two sections of a county that should never have been severed.

This part of the day's events finished, the party made its way back to Appleby to the King's Head Inn, the headquarters of the Directors.

At this point, the weather started to deteriorate, and the rain began to fall.

The next event in this day of celebration was a dinner, which followed at 2.30 pm. The venue was the ground behind the King's Head Inn and it was Admiral Elliot who presided. Lord Brougham joined the group which consisted of the men who had attended the morning proceedings, together with a number of others. In spite of 116 accepting, about 150 people dined and Mrs Winter of the King's Head provided, we are told, a 'creditable' spread which included venison sent by the Earl of Lonsdale. Apparently the champagne and wine flowed freely.

Another series of speeches was made, and toasts were drunk. In replying to a toast, the vicar of Appleby could not resist a reference to 'this other Eden' and a small meadow named Elysian Fields. He hoped the railway would not spoil the scenery and disturb the birdsong with snorting and hissing. Yet he realised the people would benefit. Coal would be cheaper, as would be lime, the latter much needed to refresh the worn-out land.

Further toasts included the Army and Navy (by William Crackanthorpe), Lord Lonsdale (in his absence, by William Brougham), the High Sheriff of the County of Westmorland (by the Chairman) and Lord Brougham (also by the Chairman).

In replying, Lord Brougham said he actually disliked travelling on the railway, but preferred the road, so that he could stop when he wished to sleep 'or for any other purpose.' However, he accepted that, as one who had time, he could take a more leisurely approach, and so his view might be seen as a selfish attitude. For many, the railways would come as a blessing. He mentioned Edward Pease MP, who had been on the original list of Directors, regretting his loss and pointing out that he and George Stephenson were mainly to thank for the success of railways. He went on to propose a toast to Mr Pease but, bearing in mind his sect (a Quaker), 'the company drank in the form of a solemn silence'.

There followed more toasts: to Sir Richard Tufton (by William Crackanthorpe), the health of the members of the county (by Mr John Crosby), the Chairman and Directors of the Eden Valley Railway, the Chairman and Directors of the Stockton and Darlington (thanking them for their assistance), the Lancaster and Carlisle, and the South Durham and Lancashire Companies. Then came the toast to the Engineer, Thomas Bouch. John Whitwell, in proposing this toast, again heaped on the praise, not least because the Engineer had 'the peculiar facility which he manifested in the manufacturing of cheap railroads, not only cheap, but ones which worked well.'

Thomas Bouch, replying, assured the company that the railway would not be a difficult one to build, and would be inexpensive.

There followed toasts to the Mayor and Corporation, the inhabitants of Appleby and also the strangers present.

Finally, a toast was proposed to the ladies.

With an abundance of fine words spoken, and much praise given in many quarters, not least to Lord Brougham, the dinner was concluded. Even so, not the festivities . . .

That evening, there was a ball at the King's Head, attended by the High Sheriff.

During the afternoon, whilst the dinner had been going on, the Oddfellows had had their own banquet in front of the Crown and Mitre Inn, the Foresters at the Coach and Horses Inn, and the scholars of St Lawrence's and St Michael's parishes were given tea (at a cost of 4d. each). A thousand children attended, with a further two thousand people who also had tea provided.

The tent used for these teas was 60 yards long, about 160 stones of bread and cake were consumed, and water was supplied in pipes laid across the road from the brewery!

An entry in the Diaries of John Sutherland, the schoolmaster at Crosby Ravensworth, who was in Appleby on the day, reads as follows:

Aug. 4th. To Appleby to see the first sod of the Eden Valley Railway cut by Lord Brougham, got a good stand but a dreadful squeezing. About 10,000 people there. Appleby finely decorated, dined at the White Heart [sic], back to Sowerby.

What a day for the people of Appleby and district. All effort was made to bring home the message that the coming of the Eden Valley Railway was of great local significance, and would bring such benefits that the day it was started should live in their memories for the rest of their lives!

Chapter Six

Construction
(1858-1866)

With the junketing over, the work proper began. The Lawton brothers, (Joseph and John) of Carlisle, were appointed the contractors, and the work was put in hand.

The contract contains a completion date agreement of 1st September, 1860.

Although Lawtons' contract included such items as coal depots, loading-bays and weigh-houses, the building of the stations was undertaken later by Nelsons, also of Carlisle, with some additional work by James Jones of Barnard Castle.

Warcop, Kirkby Thore, Temple Sowerby and Cliburn stations cost £590 each to build; Appleby cost £975 and Musgrave £220.

In fact, there had been another very competitive tender for building the line from John Anderson of Middlesbrough. In writing to the Secretary, Anderson claimed the estimate to be 'very low indeed', meeting, as it did, the requirement of £6,000 per mile with rails at £8 18s. 6d. per ton.

The method of payment which John Anderson requested was one fourth of the amount of the contract per month in paid-up shares. For every £100 of work executed, £75 in cash, £25 in shares - but debited to him at £20.

As far as the cost of rail was concerned, Anderson was well over the estimate given by John Austin and Co. of Fenchurch Street, London. In reply to an enquiry by the Secretary, a figure of £5 6s. 7d. per ton was quoted in a letter dated 14th December, 1857.

Although the line did not present any major problems, building was not as rapid as had been anticipated. The inclement Westmorland weather slowed the work down! In spite of this, the work pressed ahead.

Accidents during the building were not infrequent, although few were of a serious nature and seemed to be typified by the one reported in the *Kendal Mercury* of 26th January involving a fall of earth at Kirkby Thore on Friday 18th January when a man's leg was broken.

At a meeting of the Directors on 21st February, 1859 it was possible to report that 14 miles of land had been purchased, there had been agreement with the SD&LUR for a joint station at Kirkby Stephen and that the plans for the junction at Clifton had been put to the Directors of the L&C for approval.

By August 1859 (half-yearly meeting 8th August), the Engineer had to report that the work was behind schedule. He attributed this to the fact that large undertakings were often slow to make progress in the initial stages.

Whilst building was going ahead, developments were taking place elsewhere which would have considerable influence on the future success of the EVR. A glance at the map of the district is enough to show that what was needed to make the east-west route more effective was a further section of line westwards from the Penrith area to join with the railways on the west coast of Cumberland.

No doubt, such a glance had moved a group of individuals, in 1860, to think through a scheme which could involve building a railway from Penrith to Cockermouth, via Keswick.

27

At a meeting in the County Court Rooms, Keswick, on Saturday 23rd September, 1860, a group of people met with a view to promoting such a railway. The main object of the proposal, as outlined by Mr Waugh, at the request of the chairman H.C. Marshall, was 'to unite the railways of West Cumberland to those in the east of the County and the Eden Valley Line which communicates with the South Durham and Yorkshire Systems.' Another objective was to establish the shortest distance between the coal-yielding districts of Durham and the iron furnaces of West Cumberland, and between the haematite ores of West Cumberland and the iron furnaces of Middlesbrough and Durham.

It was pointed out that 16 blast furnaces had been or were in the course of being constructed, mainly at Workington, for which coal was procured from South Durham. It was clear to those involved that a new line would have a high financial return.

Some concern was expressed by the Maryport and Carlisle Railway, and this company backed a project to build a line from Penrith to Maryport by way of Caldbeck, this being surveyed by Mr Addison during November 1860. In the event, it was the Cockermouth, Keswick & Penrith Railway (CK&PR) which was incorporated by an Act of 1st August, 1861.

Arrangements had been made to use the LNWR station at Penrith and what was to become, in 1866, the LNWR station at Cockermouth.

The south-facing junction planned for the Penrith end of the EVR now became an impractical proposition. The CK&PR was, however, still some years away, and so the building of it went ahead. It was, in fact, to be short-lived, once a realistic route to the west was near to being realised.

The CK&PR was another of Thomas Bouch's railways, but this time, located as it was to the west of the West Coast Main Line, the LNWR had a considerable influence over it.

At a half-yearly meeting of the EVR, on 20th February, 1860, it was reported that the purchases of land had proceeded very satisfactorily and, whilst there were one or two exceptions, had been concluded. The amount received in shares up to the end of December (1859) was £45,980 with additional income of £12,394 3s. 9d.

The amount expended up to 30th June, 1859 was £16,894 14s. 8d. and, during the following six months up to the end of December, £438 1s. 6d.

In addition there were construction costs, as follows:

	£	s.	d.
Engineering	650	3	0
Land Tenants	6	18	3
Landowners	5,046	1	0
Works	£10,821	19	10
Materials	£6,537	14	3

The balance in hand was £17,806 8s. 0d. with an additional amount of interest, £182 6s. 3d.

Thomas Bouch expressed regret that progress was not as great as had been hoped. However, he was able to report that over 23 miles of permanent fencing had been erected, 185,000 cubic yards had been excavated, representing 8½ miles of line. One underbridge was complete, and 13 others were in progress, most of which were finished, apart from the girders. As far as the permanent way was concerned, about 5½ miles had been laid. Bouch was still optimistic that the line would be ready for the opening of the SD&LUR.

In fact, inclement weather had delayed work on the SD&LUR as well. Bouch, at a meeting in Northgate, Darlington, only a few days earlier, had had to express regret that line was not progressing as he had hoped.

The Chairman of the EVR seemed disappointed. He had hoped for a report which would have indicated a more advanced state to the works, but he conceded that nothing more could be done: the weather was the problem.

In spite of this, some shareholders were not satisfied with the progress and some criticism of Thomas Bouch followed. It was suggested that he had not made a proper survey before drawing up the report, and that the line was not as advanced as they were being led to believe. The target date had been fixed for 1st October, which would almost certainly not be met. Yet, in spite of the misgivings, the Directors expressed their complete confidence in Bouch.

On 2nd May, 1860 a special meeting of the Directors was held at the Castle Inn, Brough. The purpose of this meeting was to discuss arrangements 'for the vesting of the railway of this company - or otherwise amalgamating the same - with the line of the S&D.'

The Castle Inn was again the venue for a meeting on 30th August. On this occasion it was reported that about a quarter of the work on the EVR remained to be executed; that contracts for the erection of the stations had been entered into and that arrangements had also been made 'for the erection of the electric telegraph along the line'.

It was further noted that the work was behind schedule and the contractor should be urged to proceed with all haste. By this time the masonry for the bridge at Skygarth was ready for the girders, but the one at Musgrave was less advanced, flooding having caused some delay. Twenty-seven bridges were finished, or nearly so, and 2,200 rails and chairs had been delivered and 16,300 yards of track laid.

Also in August 1860, at the half-yearly meeting of the S&D, the following statement was made:

The South Durham and Eden Valley Lines are expected to be ready for mineral traffic in the present year, and for passengers early in 1861. The openings of these lines will give improved means of communication between the railways and ports on both sides of the kingdom, and, in the opinion of your Directors, will tend greatly to the further development of the trade of your district. Your Directors have entered into an agreement with each of the companies for the amalgamation of their lines with the S&DR on the terms submitted to, and approved by, the special general meeting, held on the 20th April last. A portion of the capital appertaining to these two companies stands at the disposal of this company, the appropriation of which it may be necessary shortly to bring under your notice; of this you will be duly advised. In pursuance of the negotiations referred to by the Chairman, at the half-yearly meeting, your Directors have entered into arrangements with the North Eastern Company for aiding the interests of the two companies, including the South Durham and Lancashire Union and Eden Valley Railways, in the carrying out of which parliamentary sanction may hereafter be required. It is proposed to divide the joint revenues of the two companies on the basis of the year 1852, which will give you 15¼ per cent of the joint earnings. Arrangements as regards through traffic, and division of profits arising therefrom, will commence on the 1st January next. The management of the S&D lines will, for a fixed period, remain under the charge of a committee, composed principally of the members of your present or future boards.

During February 1861, the railway suffered a minor setback. One of the leading Directors, John Crosby of Kirkby Thore, died, and was found to be insolvent. It seems the news came as a 'thunderclap', (to quote a contemporary report). The Eden Valley Railway was one of the heaviest creditors. Mr Brown, the Secretary, was called in to represent the railway's interest, although there were problems, it seems, because he was not a creditor himself. We are told that Admiral Elliot handled the whole unpleasant business with great sensitivity. Fortunately by this time, the railway was in a strong enough position to weather the incident without serious setbacks.

At the half-yearly meeting on Tuesday 26th February, 1861, it was possible to report that Skygarth viaduct was finished, apart from the painting, that Musgrave viaduct was also finished, apart from the south abutment, and that the west abutment and three piers of Coupland Beck viaduct were erected.

The stations at Cliburn, Temple Sowerby, Appleby and Warcop were almost complete and it was envisaged that a locomotive would run from Clifton to Appleby 'by the end of the week'. The Directors, in spite of this progress, expressed concern. They called, again, for a prompt and speedy completion, 'in justice to the shareholders.'

It was reported that a Bill was before Parliament to carry out the agreement existing between the EVR and the S&D by which the former would be amalgamated with the latter. Further, it was noted:

Bills having been introduced into Parliament by another Railway Company seeking for running and other powers in connection with this Railway of an objectionable character, the Directors (with the co-operation of the S&D) have deemed it necessary to appear as opponents.

(The company being referred to was the West Hartlepool Harbour and Railway Company).

Admiral Elliot retired at this meeting but was re-elected. John Crosby, Junior, resigned.

Contemporary Press reports during the period of building occasionally open windows which enable us to glimpse back at some of the minor day-to-day trials and tribulations associated with the construction of the line.

For example, on Monday 23rd April, 1861, Lawtons had to deal with an incident in Kirkby Stephen when a wagon carrying a 'locomotive engine' destined for the EVR broke the covering of the main sewer, and wagon and engine 'were thrown broadside onto the pavement'. No real damage was done and nobody was injured. It was possible, later the same day, to deliver the engine.

In contrast to minor mishaps, another event was a matter for considerable celebration. Joseph Lawton (one of the contractors) fell in love with Arabella Fairer of Warcop and on 30th January, 1861 they were married. Before the ceremony, the men working on the railway joined in a special celebration.

The SD&LUR was eventually opened to mineral traffic in July 1861, and to passengers the following month. It was possible to report in the *Kendal Mercury* of 6th July that the first cargo of Durham coal for Kendal had arrived on 'Thursday last', and had been consigned to Mr George Gaskell.

The EVR, in spite of Bouch's optimism, did not meet the target of opening at the same time. On Tuesday 15th October a locomotive and carriage was able to traverse the whole of the line in order to convey the Directors for the purpose of carrying out an inspection. Optimistic that the line would be open for mineral traffic by Christmas and passengers early in January, they gave instructions to the contractors to speed up the ballasting of the line. However it was into 1862 before the line was ready for traffic. Mineral trains started running on 8th April. Passengers had to wait rather longer. The Government Inspector, Captain Tyler, visited during the early part of May 1862.

By this time, there had been some heavy goods trains, but as far as local traffic was concerned, for example between Penrith and Appleby, it appears that the road hauliers were able to hold their own and carry goods at a much cheaper rate.

It was reported that 'in the coal trade the promised blessings are yet to come, for up to the present time there has been little difference between buying at the station (in Appleby) or carting the same from Penrith.'

On the occasion of his first visit, on 4th May, Captain Tyler was accompanied by Thomas Bouch. Some aspects were found wanting, especially on one or two of the bridges. Strengthening of Skygarth viaduct was necessary. As mentioned previously, it had four spans. These were 105 feet from centre to centre and although the piers and abutments were built by the main contractors, Lawtons, the metal superstructure had been constructed by Kenlard and Company of London. Because there was a need for this additional work, passenger traffic could not commence, although the mineral trains continued to run.

Some delay may well have been caused by the fact that the Lawton Brothers were finding it difficult to get payments out of the company.

On 1st July, 1862, John Lawton wrote to the Secretary:

> I am under the disagreeable necessity of again applying to you for the advance of two thousand pounds on account of the work executed on the Eden Valley Railway. My former application to you for the aforementioned amount was made on 4th June and I have now to request you to call a Board meeting to grant me the amount by Friday . . . This must positively be done . . . I cannot go on any longer without an advance . . . I cannot see why any objections can be made against this application.

The writer explains that the bills due against the firm the previous week had all been dishonoured and the monthly pay put off for the EVR. 'This has caused great annoyance.' He concludes, 'I cannot properly be put off any longer.

John Lawton (for the Lawton brothers).'

A problem now began to loom large. It had been anticipated that the railway would be open by the time the fairs were held, and these would start on 9th July. It will be remembered that serving the fairs had been specifically mentioned when the railway had been projected. Time was getting short.

At this point, William Hopes, the Vice-Chairman, brought pressure to bear, and as a result the problems were rectified. By 7th June, the line was ready to open for passengers. It is reported that Captain Tyler inferred when giving the go-ahead that he had not come across a line which did as much credit to those involved in planning and building it as the Eden Valley Line.

The opening on Saturday 7th June did not have the grand celebrations which had accompanied the cutting of the first sod. Instead, a train was run from Kirkby Stephen to Clifton and back. It had several carriages and stopped at all the stations on the line. Anybody who wished to take a ride could do so free of charge.

A number of Directors were present, including William Hopes and James Atkinson, together with groups from the SD&LUR and the S&D.

After travelling the line, they stopped off at Appleby and, in the customary fashion, went off to the King's Head Hotel, where they enjoyed 'an excellent dinner'. On this occasion, William Hopes presided, as Admiral Elliot was not able to be present.

With virtually no time to spare, the railway was ready to cater for the fairs, which started the following Monday and lasted until Thursday. A large number of traders and visitors used the line, and on the Wednesday, the principal day, special trains travelled from Appleby to Clifton and Kirkby Stephen. Large numbers of cattle wagons were also made available, and the railway made a big impact at what was an important event in the local calendar.

There was a special meeting of the Directors (at the King's Head, Kirkby Stephen) on Thursday 29th August, 1861 for the approval of the working agreement between the EVR and S&D, subject to any alterations deemed necessary by the Board of Trade. This meeting was adjourned and reconvened on Thursday 7th November, this time at the King's Head, Appleby, when, with William Hopes in the chair, final approval was given.

At the half-yearly meeting on 13th February, 1862 it was reported that the Bill for the amalgamation was in Parliament (together with the Bill which would give more direct access to Penrith).

Yet another extraordinary meeting was held on 31st May, 1862 when the Bill for amalgamation of the SD&LUR, the EVR and the S&D was approved with an adjournment, again, awaiting developments.

By the half-yearly meeting on 5th August, 1862 (at the King's Head, Barnard Castle) it was possible to report that the Bill for amalgamation had gone through, together with the Bill for the extension and running powers over the LNWR at Clifton.

This meeting on 5th August, 1862 was the last of the EVR Board.

The S&D now took over the SD&LUR, together with the Eden Valley Line. In fact, it was not very long before the North Eastern Railway would, in turn, move in to gain control.

Chapter Seven

Further Developments

A number of moves now took place which completed the east-west link and made it an effective route. The south-facing junction, built to ensure that the railway had an essentially local function, would clearly become redundant with the arrival of the CK&PR. Instead, a northerly junction would be necessary. By an Act (Vict. Reg., 25 & 26, Cap. cxviii), passed on 7th July, 1862, the railway was empowered to build such a junction. The Act is headed 'An Act to enable the Eden Valley Railway Company to construct certain Extension and Branch Railways; to use Portions of other Railways; to raise additional Capital; and for other purposes.' It is interesting to note that although this Act came a month after the first passenger train had run on the EVR, it still contains the words 'And whereas a great Portion of the said Railway is completed but no Part thereof is yet open to traffic . . .'

Originally, there was a scheme to run a line parallel to the LNWR line into Penrith, crossing the LNWR at one point, but having gained running powers over the LNWR, such duplication proved unnecessary, and a junction was made some three miles south of Penrith.

Some correspondence about the two junctions is worthy of mention. It indicates both were, at various stages and for a number of reasons, sensitive issues for the LNWR in spite of agreements in principle.

On 28th April, 1860, Mr W. Channey wrote from Lancaster on behalf of the LNWR to George Brown of the EVR about the southerly junction. There was concern that materials belonging to the EVR were in very close proximity to the up line at Clifton and in view of the fact that horses and wagons were working in the vicinity, the LNWR had decided to put up a temporary fence to avoid accidents. Mr Channey pointed out that with the movement of materials it would be necessary to employ a look-out and a charge for this would be made to the EVR!

In a letter of 30th April the EVR queried this but on 2nd May, Mr Channey wrote again pointing out that originally two temporary watchmen had been put on at the junction on 5th May, 1859 and then taken off on 5th October. Nobody had been on duty since, until 28th April (1860) when the one man, mentioned, was put on.

The EVR clearly felt uneasy about the motives of the LNWR in this incident.

On 9th January, 1861 a letter was sent to Thomas Bouch by Mr S.B. Worthington, also at Lancaster, requesting a reply to an earlier letter, sent on 15th December, 1860. These letters concern the level at which the EVR proposed to place an engine shed, in relation 'to the level of the rails at the junction with our line'. It goes on, 'As far as I can judge . . . I should suppose the rails will be about 3 feet above our rails at the junction in which case we must make our tank which will be at the junction, 3 feet higher than we had proposed'.

On 10th May, 1862, The Articles of Agreement giving running powers to the EVR over LNWR rails between Clifton and Penrith, were sanctioned and this led to the plan for a separate line into Penrith being abandoned.

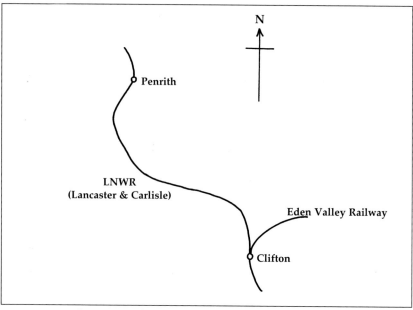

The original scheme with the south-facing junction (1862)

The north-facing junction (1863)

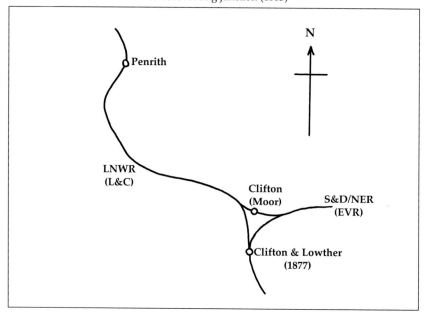

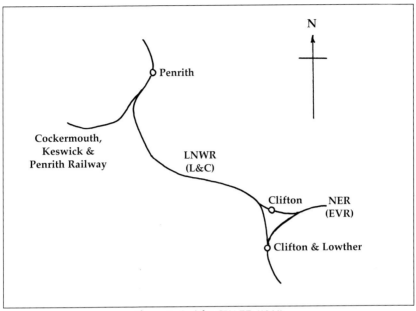

The arrival of the CK&PR (1864)

The final stage. The link from the LNWR at Eamont to the CK&PR at Red Hills (1866)

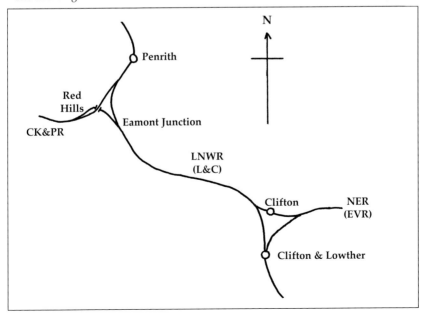

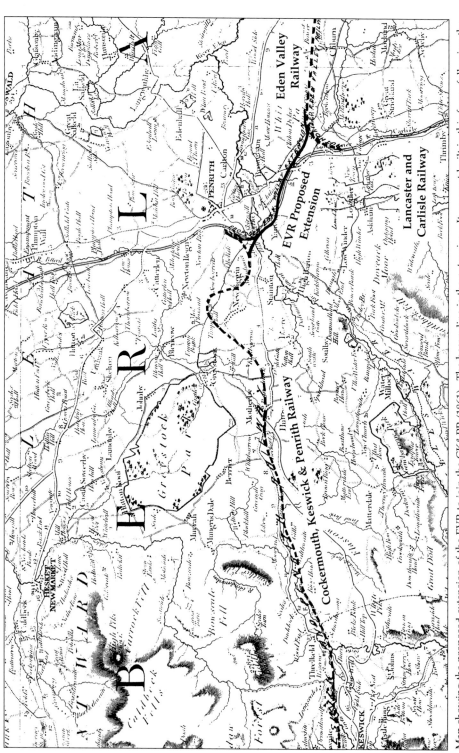

Map showing the proposed extension of the EVR to join the CK&PR (1861). The heavy line is the extension. It was not built in this form, following the granting of running powers over the LNWR.

Cumbria Record Office

However, on 11th June, 1863 a letter from William Cawkwell (no less) at Euston was sent to George Brown expressing grave concern about the nature of the northerly junction.

It was always supposed that such connection would be made in a manner and possessing such gradients as would not interfere with or endanger the safe working of the London N.W. Line [*sic*]. I had not the most distant idea of a proposition being made like that which your engineer suggests of constructing a curved line on a falling gradient of 1 in 56. If such a thing had been intimated to us when the agreement was under discussion, I, for one, should never have consented to it and I am sure no other officer nor any Director connected with the company would for one moment have entertained such a proposition. If your engineer could alter the branch so as to get rid of the objectionable gradient, no opposition will be offered on the part of this company to the formation of the junction, although I am still of the opinion, which expressed at the time the agreement was under discussion, that such a junction is not really necessary and that the traffic could be better worked by means of a single junction now in the course of construction.

The spur was built quickly. It opened in August 1863 in readiness for the opening of the CK&PR, which followed in November 1864. By an Act of June 1863, the LNWR and the S&D each subscribed £25,000 and obtained agreements regarding the working of the CK&PR.

Once the CK&PR was open and the southern junction had no practical purpose, powers were sought to abandon it. The Act for this received the Royal Assent on 16th July, 1874, under an Additional Powers Act (Vict. Reg. 37 & 38, Cap. cxxxiv). This was obtained by the North Eastern Railway which took over the S&D in the latter part of 1863. As a result of these changes, Clifton station on the original junction was eventually renamed Clifton and Lowther, and a new station was opened on the northern spur to the east of Clifton village.

With this junction in place, the only section which needed to be addressed was one to link the LNWR with the CK&PR in a way which would remove the need for trains to reverse at Penrith. In an Act (Vict. Reg. 27 & 28, Cap. lxvii) which received the Royal Assent on 23rd June, 1864, the NER received powers to build a section of line from Eamont Junction to Red Hills, on the CK&PR.

The CK&PR opened to freight in November 1864. The spur opened for traffic in September 1866. So the east-west link was complete. It provided facilities which the original promoters of the Eden Valley Line doubtless could hardly have imagined.

Through traffic could flow along the Eden Valley and pass directly westwards to Cumberland in what was an effective direct route.

As far as operations were concerned, the NER had control over the section from the east to the Eden Valley Junction. On the CK&PR, the passenger and general goods traffic was operated by the LNWR and the mineral traffic by the NER, an arrangement which suited the latter admirably.

In 1863 there were two passenger trains in each direction each day, one in the morning and one mid-afternoon. An additional earlier train was run from Kirkby Stephen on Tuesdays only. At this stage, before the completion of the northern junction, it was necessary to change at Clifton (Clifton and Lowther, as it was to become, later). Once the northerly junction was in use, following its opening at the beginning of August 1863, trains could operate in and out of Penrith. At the beginning of 1864 there were two trains in each direction between Kirkby Stephen and Penrith, one in the morning and one in the afternoon.

The timing made it possible to operate the service with one train, the outline being as follows: depart Kirkby Stephen 8.40 am (this time varies slightly over a period), arrive Penrith 9.35 am. Depart Penrith 9.45 am and arrive Kirkby Stephen at 10.55 am.

The afternoon train left Kirkby Stephen at 2.30, arrived at Penrith at 3.25 pm, left again at 3.35, and arrived back in Kirkby Stephen at 4.30 pm.

The morning trains stopped at all stations; the afternoon trains stopped at all stations except Musgrave.

On Mondays only an additional down train was introduced between Appleby and Kirkby Stephen, leaving Appleby at 1 pm, and arriving at Kirkby Stephen at 1.25.

During 1864, a number of variations appear to have been tried. These included changing the timings slightly and then, in April, introducing a Mondays-only up train, leaving Kirkby Stephen at 5.20 pm.

By July, a third up train was introduced, leaving Kirkby Stephen at 5.30 pm, and arriving at Penrith at 6.27. This was complemented by a third down train, leaving Penrith at 6.50 and arriving at Kirkby Stephen at 7.45 pm.

The Mondays-only up train was taken off at this stage. All the up trains stopped at all stations with one exception. This time it was not Musgrave that missed out, but Cliburn.

The last train of the day, which left Penrith at 5.45 pm did not stop at Cliburn, Clifton or Musgrave. The Mondays-only down train was retained.

By January 1865, the service had become two up trains and two down trains, and the pattern was retained for the rest of the year.

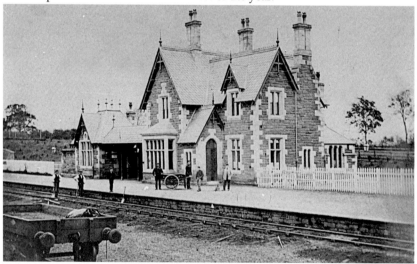

Appleby around the date of opening showing uncompleted ballasting.

John Mallon Collection

Chapter Eight

Enter the Midland
(1876-1893)

A little further south from the Vale of Eden, the Vale of Lune had been a far less tranquil place as far as railway politics were concerned. A whole series of plans and counter-plans had been devised. These involved chiefly the Lancaster and Carlisle, the North Western (the so-called 'Little North Western', to distinguish it from the London & North Western) and later the LNWR and the Midland. These companies became locked in a dispute about the making of a railway through this part of the Yorkshire Dales. Eventually, the Ingleton branch (or Lune Valley Railway) was built. This was intended as a through route from the West Riding to Scotland but the scheme fell foul of the LNWR which had no intention of allowing the Midland proper access or connections on to the West Coast Main Line at Lowgill and thence to Scotland.

For a period of years, the LNWR pursued obstructionist policies, trying the patience of the Midland to the limit. In the end, the Midland Company decided that the only satisfactory solution to the problem of gaining entry to Carlisle was to build its own line.

The story of the Settle and Carlisle (S&C) has been told many times. The Midland instructed Crossley, its Engineer, to plan a route over some of the most difficult terrain in the country. After the subsequent backing down by the LNWR, the Midland then decided to abandon its scheme. This plan to abandon was met by considerable opposition by a number of railway companies. It is of interest to note that, at this stage, Admiral Elliot once again enters the arena. Having worked so hard to get a railway for Appleby he was delighted at the proposal that a second railway would serve the town.

News that the Midland had decided to seek Parliamentary approval to abandon the project did not meet with his approval. He set about drumming up local support to oppose the possible abandonment and a committee was formed, of which he became Chairman, to discuss a suitable course of action. At a meeting in the Crown Hotel, Penrith, on Tuesday 12th February, 1869, at which William Hopes was also present, it was agreed to make a submission to Parliament, setting out, from the point of view of people living in the Vale of Eden, why the Midland should not be allowed to abandon its scheme.

After lengthy proceedings during April, Parliament decided the Midland must go ahead and build, much to the dismay of the LNWR but to the satisfaction of a number of other railway companies - and Russell Elliot!

The type of battle fought in the Vale of Lune was not fought in the Vale of Eden.

Although the NER had kept a wary eye on a number of schemes proposed for the Dales, which would possibly link to the North-East, and had, in one case, had to move in and buy out the scheme to remove the threat, it was anxious to befriend the Midland as it became more and more apparent that it would be its new neighbour in the vale.

The proposals by the Midland had, at one stage, involved the possibility of using part of the Eden Valley Line, but in the end the Midland decided to make its own way to Carlisle along the Eden Valley. The two railways would be near neighbours at Appleby.

When the Midland line opened in 1876, Russell Elliot was still alive and very active and able to witness the event. He died five years later on 28th December, 1881, quite suddenly of a heart attack, although his health had been failing for some time. In typical manner, he had spent the morning arranging for several tons of coal (no doubt brought in by the EVR!) to be distributed to the poor in Appleby. He was buried at St Lawrence's Church in the town.

In view of the proximity of the two lines and the fact that the Midland beyond Appleby was to go in a north-westerly direction to Carlisle, whilst the EVR went in a westerly direction to Penrith, junctions between the two railways were planned in the original Midland proposals. The NER had no objection to these.

It appears that only one of the two proposed junctions was connected to the EVR. This was a westward-facing one which enabled trains to travel from the Midland station (Appleby West) on to the EVR and thence to Penrith. Such a connection would enable the running of a Lake District service and these would be able to compete with a similar service run over the Ingleton branch.

After the S&C opened for traffic the Midland was quick to approach the NER with a view to introducing a Lake District link from Appleby. Discussions took place in July 1878, but in August the idea was dropped. However, it was later revived, and in July 1880 three additional trains appeared in the EVR timetable. These connected Appleby (Midland) with Penrith.

The *Railway News* of 21st August, 1880 contains the following report:

Additional expresses have been arranged to bring the Northern and Midland Counties of England into more direct access to Bristol, Bath and Bournemouth and the South and West of England generally; and the stopping of the express at Appleby and a fresh service of trains between Appleby and Penrith put the vast populations resident on the main line of Midland in immediate communication with Keswick and the Northern part of the Lake District.

However, towards the end of 1893, 13 years later, these trains were dropped and a local service of five trains a day, stopping at all stations, was all that remained.

Details of this change are shown in the timetables reproduced elsewhere.

During this period, on Saturday evening, 14th January, 1882, a most horrific accident occurred near Clifton station when a book and cloth traveller named W.P. Muse from Carlisle was hit by a train and his body very badly mutilated. In the account of the accident it is assumed he was run down by 'the Midland express from Appleby'; a reference, no doubt, to the through train to Penrith which had left Appleby at 5.50 pm.

Chapter Nine

The Middle Years
(1893-1952)

After this brief flirtation with the Midland, the Eden Valley Line settled down to a pattern of existence which, although it varied in minor ways from time to time, remained essentially the same for the next 60 years until closure proposals began to loom.

There is a familiar sequence found frequently in the stories of many lines resembling the Eden Valley; a vigorous campaign to establish a company and then build, a period of steady operation, with, perhaps, some expansion and then a second, equally vigorous campaign to fight off closure once that threat becomes evident.

Timetable patterns, after the dropping of the Midland link from Appleby to Penrith, change very little. There were five trains each way, at times which vary little; two morning trains, two afternoon trains and one evening train. It may be of interest to note that, for a time, after the trains from Appleby Midland were discontinued, some timetables had an unusual feature; columns headed 'M' for trains to and from Appleby Midland; the columns are empty! Perhaps there was a feeling these trains would reappear.

In some years, slight variations were sometimes introduced during the summer months, but this type of modification is spasmodic and by and large very inconsistent.

The Eden Valley Line had many aspects of a branch line in that it had a very local element in its character, serving, as it did, the small towns and communities which lay along its route.

The people who worked the line were, in many cases, local people or people who became well known in the locality.

'Long Harry' was such a person. Henry Walton, to give him his proper name, was a popular guard who had joined the EVR when it opened; in fact he had been on duty on the first train. We are told he was a man with a keen sense of humour who could crack a joke with anyone without degenerating into coarseness; he was genial and kind and to know him was to like him. He worked on the EVR until about 1888 and then moved to Darlington when his duties took him into that part of the world. When he collapsed and died in September 1894 whilst on duty on a train travelling towards Bowes, his death was mourned in a wide area of the Eden Valley and numerous people attended his funeral.

Later, the line saw the presence of the Sykes brothers. Mr J.M. Sykes and Mr L. Sykes worked together as driver and fireman during the 1920s. A splendid water colour was painted showing a Fletcher 2-4-0 of the '1440' class in the green livery of the NER and of which they were acting as crew, leaving Penrith on the 10.22 am for Kirkby Stephen.

Mr J.M. Sykes' son, Mr C.R. Sykes, also joined the railway, becoming a top link driver on the East Coast Main Line and, later, a locomotive foreman at Newcastle.

Station.	Single Fares 1st s. d.	Single Fares 2nd s. d.	Single Fares 3rd s. d.	Single Fares Parl s. d.	Return Fares 1st s. d.	Return Fares 2nd s. d.	Return Fares 3rd s. d.
Accrington	17 6	12 8	7 9	7 4½	29 3	20 6	15 6
Appleby	2 8	2 0		1 2	4 6	3 4	2 0
Barnard Castle	8 8	6 6		4 0	14 6	11 0	6 9
Barrow-in-Furness	15 1	10 6	6 6	6 1½	24 2	17 0	
Bay Horse	11 9	8 0	5 0	4 9	19 9	13 6	10 0
Belfast	19 9	15 9		9 0	32 0	26 0	15 0
Bishop Auckland	11 3	8 6		5 3	18 6	14 3	
Blackpool	17 9	12 6	8 0	7 6½	29 9	20 9	
Carlisle	3 4	2 6	1 6½	1 5¼	6 0	4 0	3 1
Carnforth	9 0	6 3	4 0	3 9	15 0	10 6	8 0
Cliburn	1 3	11		6½	2 1	1 7	11
Clifton	1 0	6	4	3½	1 8	10	7
Cockermouth	6 5	3 11		2 6½	9 8	5 10	5 1
Darlington (Bank Top)	11 10	8 9	5 9	5 5	19 10	14 9	9 2
Douglas (by Barrow)	18 6	15 0	8 6		29 9	25 9	15 10
Dublin	39 9	28 6	13 6		66 6	47 6	23 6
Edinburgh	21 4	15 0	9 10½		34 3	25 0	17 4
Fleetwood	17 9	12 6	8 2	7 8½	29 3	20 9	15 0
Furness Abbey	14 3	9 11	6 2½	5 10	23 0	16 0	
Harrowgate	19 0	14 2		8 10½	31 9	23 9	15 9
Kendal	7 0	4 10	3 1	2 10½	11 9	8 3	6 2
Kirkby Stephen	4 6	3 6		2 1	7 6	6 0	3 6
Keswick	3 9	2 3		1 6	5 8	3 5	3 0
Kirkbythore	1 9	1 4		9½	2 11	2 3	1 4
Lancaster	10 6	7 3	4 6	4 3	17 6	12 3	9 0
Liverpool	20 0	14 3	8 11	8 5	33 6	23 9	17 10
London (Euston Sta.)	38 10	30 6	22 7		76 6	60 3	45 2
Manchester (Vict. Sta)	18 0	14 0	9 1	8 7	33 6	23 6	18 2
Morecambe (Poulton)	10 6	7 3	4 6	4 3	17 6	12 3	9 0
Maryport	8 9	5 8	3 5	3 7	13 8	8 10	
Newcastle-on-Tyne	14 0	10 6		6 6	23 6	17 6	
Oxenholme	6 6	4 6	2 11	2 8½	11 0	7 6	5 10
Paris (by Dieppe)	71 10	54 6	39 7		131 6	99 3	75 2
Preston	14 6	10 0	6 5	6 0½	24 3	16 9	12 10
Plumpton	1 0	9	5½	5	1 8	1 3	11
Redcar	15 4	11 6		7 2	25 9	19 3	12 9
Saltburn	16 2	12 2		7 7	27 0	20 6	13 6
Scarboro'	24 3	18 2	12 2	11 5½	40 6	30 6	24 4
Shap	2 6	1 6	1 1	1 0	4 3	2 6	2 2
Tebay	4 0	2 9	1 8	1 7	6 9	4 9	3 4
Templesowerby	1 6	1 1		8	2 6	1 10	1 2
Troutbeck	2 0	1 3		9½	3 0	1 11	1 7
Warcop	3 6	2 8		1 7	6 0	4 6	2 8
Windermere	8 9	6 1	3 10	3 6½	14 9	10 3	7 8
Whitehaven	9 6	6 0	3 11	3 10	14 8	9 4	
York	19 4	14 6	9 7	9 1	32 3	24 3	19 2

Fares table produced in the 1890s.

North Eastern Railway.	mrn	mrn	mrn	aft	aft	aft	aft		✶ EDEN VALLEY BRANCH.	mrn	mrn	aft	aft	aft	aft	aft
Carlisle	6 50	9 30	1130		1 50		5 38		KIRKBY STEPHEN dp.	8 32	1150	..	2 15	4 25	..	6 30
PENRITH dep	7 27	1047	1245	1 43	3 53	5 20	6 40		Musgrave	8 40	1158	..	2 23	4 33	..	6 38
Clifton	7 35	1055	C	1 51	4 1	..	6 48		Warcop	8 45	12 3	..	2 28	4 38	A	6 43
Cliburn	7 41	11 1	..	1 57	4 7	..	6 54		Appleby	8 56	1214	1 25	2 39	4 49	5 50	6 55
Temple Sowerby	7 45	11 5	A	2 1	4 11	..	6 58		Kirkby Thore	9 4	1222	..	2 47	4 57	..	7 8
Kirkby Thore	7 49	11 9	..	2 5	4 15	7 3			Temple Sowerby	9 9	1227	..	2 52	5 2	..	7 13
Appleby	7 58	1118	1 10	2 14	4 24	5 45	7 16		Cliburn	9 14	1233	..	2 57	5 7	..	
Warcop	8 8	1128	..	2 24	4 34	..	7 25		Clifton	9 21	1239	..	3 4	5 14	..	7 23
Musgrave	8 13	1133	..	..	4 43	..	7 29		PENRITH arr.	9 29	1247	1 50	3 12	5 22	6 15	7 31
KIRKBY STEPHEN arr	8 21	1141	..	2 39	4 51	..	7 38		Carlisle arr	1145	2 45	..	4 10	6 10	..	8 15

Passenger timetable for December 1893.

There also grew up within the railway community of Penrith and surrounding district a great sense of 'bonhomie'. This community included the men who worked for the LNWR and CK&PR as well as the NER.

In 1890 the first of a long series of annual staff dinners was held. These dinners took the form of a 'get-together' with a meal, after-dinner speakers and entertainment by way of songs. It seems the first of these gatherings was held in the Market Hall at Tebay at the instigation of a clergyman, and involved only clerical staff.

By 1894, the event had moved to Penrith and all groups of railway employees were invited, the cost being met by 'the liberal subscriptions of the gentry resident in the town and neighbourhood.' About a hundred men attended in 1894, and these included station masters, clerks, guards, porters and platelayers.

The mood of these events can be gleaned, in part, from the banter that took place. In 1894, during his address and when referring to the various railway companies involved, the Chairman, H.C. Howard, caused laughter and cheering by making the following comment:

> The North Eastern is also a very important connection which only has one fault which I hope, when I have mentioned it, will no longer continue. The North Eastern will never wait for the trains on the CK&PR although they always make the trains of that company wait for theirs!

(The response to a similar comment, had Midland and LNWR men from Ingleton been present, hardly bears thinking about!)

An observation was made about the absence of ladies at the dinner and the hope expressed that before long they too would be included.

One speaker suggested this might come about because lady engine drivers would soon be found working alongside the men, although in reply the Chairman, whilst having no doubt about the competence of ladies in charge of engines, did hope they would be careful about not going too fast down Shap incline!

At the 21st dinner in January 1910, there were some 130 employees present. The mood was jovial but some reservations were creeping into the speeches. These concerned shrinking trade and the competition of the motor car; about 'gigantic cars distributing goods in London which used to go by train' and the introduction of electric trams in many areas.

These fears of competition from road transport are aired time after time in numerous gatherings and meetings. Not, in fact, without good reason.

Twelve years later, on Friday 20th June, 1922, the children of Warcop school were given a special treat; a day in Blackpool. They left Warcop at 6.30 am, and did not get home until 1 am on Saturday morning! They went on the sands; some went on a sailing boat and then all visited the Tower, where they were admitted free of charge. The Pleasure Beach was the next call and then, after buying souvenirs, they set off for home at 7.30 pm. The significant feature of this trip was that the children were not taken by train; they travelled by charabanc which enabled them to stop off and see various places of interest *en route*.

Fears were being realised; a competitor to rail travel was beginning to emerge

A general view of Penrith station in LNWR days.   *Lens of Sutton*

Eden Valley Junction in 1903 showing the LNWR signal box and points set and signal pulled off
for a train passing onto the Eden Valley Line.   *L&GRP*

Two views of Clifton in the early part of the century. The station is seen above and the lower view is of the station master's house. This station was renamed Clifton Moor on 1st September, 1927 to avoid confusion with the ex-LNWR station on the West Coast main line Clifton and Lowther which also served the village.   *Penrith Library*

Above: A view from the early part of this century at Kirkby Thore.

North Road Museum

Right: Kirkby Thore looking east. The local train is hauled by a Tennant '1463' class. Note the token exchange is about to take place.

North Road Museum

Below: A '901' class 2-4-0 pauses at Appleby in NER days.

Lens of Sutton

Warcop looking east *c.* 1918 showing the original signal box. *John Mallon Collection*

Kirkby Stephen station looking west. *Lens of Sutton*

ARMSTRONG & SIDDLES'
Motor and Transport Co.
LIMITED

13, Middlegate, Penrith.

MOTOR
SALOON BUS SERVICE

between PENRITH and APPLEBY
and vice versa,

Commencing on 1st JANUARY, 1924,
until further notice.

Motor leaves	Daily. a.m.	Daily. p.m.	Sat. only. p.m.
PENRITH, 13, Middlegate	9–15	4–15	9– 0
Carleton	9–20	4–20	9– 5
Lightwater	9–25	4–25	9–10
Whinfell School	9–30	4–30	9–15
Winderwath	9–35	4–35	9–20
Culgaith Road	9–40	4–40	9–25
Templesowerby	9–43	4–43	9–28
Kirkbythore	9–50	4–50	9–35
Longmarton	9–55	4–55	9–40
Crackenthorpe	10– 5	5– 5	9–50
APPLEBY	10–15	5–15	10– 0

Motor leaves	Daily. a.m.	Daily. p.m.	Sat. only. p.m.
APPLEBY	8– 0	3– 0	5–15
Crackenthorpe	8–10	3–10	5–25
Longmarton	8–15	3–15	5–30
Kirkbythore	8–20	3–20	5–35
Templesowerby	8–30	3–30	5–45
Culgaith Road	8–33	3–33	5–48
Winderwath	8–40	3–40	5–55
Whinfell School	8–45	3–45	6– 0
Lightwater	8–50	3–50	6– 5
Carleton	8–55	3–55	6–10
PENRITH, Middlegate	9– 0	4– 0	6–15

Penrith.
```
3d. Carleton
5d.............3d. Lightwater
7d.........................3d. Whinfell School
9d................................3d. Winderwath
1/-..........................................3d. Templesowerby
1/2...............................................3d. Kirkbythore
1/5.....................................................3d. Crackenthorpe
1/8..........................................................3d. Appleby
```

RETURN TICKETS.

Penrith to Appleby, or vice versa	3/3
Penrith or Appleby to Templesowerby, or vice versa	1/10
Penrith to Kirkbythore, or vice versa	2/3
Appleby to Kirkbythore, or vice versa	1/4

ALL PARCELS TO BE PAID FOR IN ADVANCE.

Parcels from Penrith to be handed in at BOOKING OFFICE, 13, MIDDLEGATE, where Waiting Room is also provided.

Appleby Parcels should be Left at G. S. EVANS'S SHOP.

The Proprietors give notice that they do not undertake that the Motors shall start or arrive at the times specified in the Company's time bills, nor will they be responsible for any loss, inconvenience or injury which may arise from delays or from any cause whatever.

JOHN KIDD,
Managing Director and Secretary.

as a real threat to the future of the railway; in this case the EVR in particular.

In December 1923, 18 months later, Armstrong and Siddles Motor and Transport Company of Penrith announced that on 1st January, 1924 they would introduce a 'saloon bus service' between Penrith and Appleby. There would be two journeys each way on weekdays; Penrith (depart) 9.15 am and 4.15 pm; Appleby (depart) 8.00 am; and 3.00 pm, with an additional journey each way on Saturdays; Appleby (depart) 5.15 pm, Penrith (depart) 9.00 pm. This made it possible to have an 'evening out' in Penrith on Saturdays. The journey time was one hour, the return fare for the whole journey was 3s. 3d. (this was a penny less than a second class return fare on the railway; first class 4s. 6d., third class 2s.). There were a good number of intermediate stops with fares graded accordingly. In addition to carrying passengers, who, incidentally, were provided with a waiting room at Penrith, parcels were also conveyed.

Mr John Kidd, the Managing Director, was confident the venture would be a success.

The introduction of this type of service was not good news for the EVR. The railways found it hard to compete over such short haul routes and the greater convenience in terms of flexibility which the motor coaches offered was very attractive to passengers.

Following this incursion by a local bus company, the introduction of motor bus services moved on with vigorous pace during the 1920s. Competition became fierce, ending, sometimes, in the court room, where accusations of reckless driving and obstruction became quite common as the companies vied to outdo each other. Advertising in the local press was very prominent as this new form of transport gained a greater hold on the market. The remarkable thing is that the railway seemed unmoved by it all. Rarely did it advertise its services in an attempt to counter the growing tide of bus operators. Perhaps it just assumed it was there to be used and everyone knew that was so; perhaps there was a sense of apathy, too. Few advertisements were placed for special excursions which involved the EVR, the LNER taking the occasional small entry, unlike the LMS which regularly brought to the attention of readers of the local press the numerous special offers and excursions being run. Later, the LNER was to be criticised for not pursuing a more active policy in this respect. If it had done so, things might have turned out differently.

There had been pleas for improved services. At the beginning of December 1923, the Westmorland County Council received resolutions from Kirkby Stephen Parish Council, the Federation of Women's Institutes and the Appleby Town Council urging the necessity for 'more convenient railway communication between North and East and South Westmorland.'

Mr A.H. Willink proposed a motion that 'the attention of the London and North Eastern Railway Company be called to the matter with a request that much better facilities be provided and that it is strongly urged that as a minimum improvement the train which formerly ran from Kirkby Stephen to Kendal in connection with the 10.51 am train from Appleby be reinstated and particularly there should be a train run from Tebay to Kirkby Stephen on Mondays, Fridays and Saturdays to link up with the train leaving Tebay at 1.45 pm with the train now leaving Kirkby Stephen at 2.40 pm for Appleby and Penrith.'

The challenge to the railway came from the bus services introduced in the early 1920s. This postcard view by Atkinson and Pollitt almost certainly shows a vehicle belonging to Armstrong and Siddles, who introduced a service from Penrith to Appleby in 1924 and later extended it to Kirkby Stephen. The location is the Countess' Pillar on the A66. Note the complete absence of other traffic. The competition from the motor car was yet to come!   *John Marsh Collection*

General view of Kirkby Stephen yard, looking east in June 1935. The coaching stock is particularly interesting.   *H.C. Casserley*

Ex-GNR 'D3' class 4-4-0 No. 4346 stands at Kirkby Stephen with a Darlington-Penrith train in June 1935. *H.C. Casserley*

Kirkby Stephen Shed on 5th June, 1935. 'J25' class 0-6-0 No. 1994 can be seen outside the shed along with 'J21' 0-6-0 No. 147, inside the shed 'G5' class 0-4-4T No. 1916 can be distinguished. *H.C. Casserley*

There appears to have been no substantial response to this proposal.

Meanwhile, the competition from the bus companies heightened. By 1928 the Great North of England Bus Service (a name which seems to emulate those of the railway companies!) was operating a service from Carlisle to Darlington via Penrith, Temple Sowerby, Bolton, Appleby and Brough, virtually in direct competition with the EVR and the extended service to Darlington which had been introduced at the turn of the century.

There were three buses a day each way on this service and, for example, it was possible to leave Penrith at 10.30 am and be in Darlington for 1.30 pm. Leaving Darlington at 4.30 pm enabled a traveller to be back in Penrith by 7.30 pm. (There was also a special 'Theatre Bus' for Carlisle.) It was a long time on the bus for only three hours in Darlington but as roads and vehicles improved so these improvements were to be reflected in better services. What is more, this service connected with others to all parts of Yorkshire, Durham, Northumberland and West Cumberland.

In 1929 Armstrong and Siddles, with services by this time reaching from Penrith to Carlisle, Appleby and Kirkby Stephen, became part of the mighty 'Ribble' empire as it forged north from its beginnings in Preston in 1919. Ribble had absorbed numerous small companies to establish a powerful company consolidating bus services and linking with other groups to give a comprehensive service. Some railway companies, sensing mounting opposition, sought to buy shares in bus companies in order to try and influence events and in 1930 the railways welcomed the Road Traffic Act which, they felt, could well retard or hinder the growth of bus traffic. Under the Act certain restrictions could be applied and the railway companies, along with others, had an opportunity to raise objections to proposed services. The tide, however, could not be turned, as competition intensified.

At around this time, the LNER did make a move to attract the attention of the public and semi-display, single column advertisements appeared for special excursions from Penrith and Appleby to Newcastle, Tynemouth and Whitley Bay, in effect reaching further than the bus companies were able to do, as far as this sort of traffic was concerned.

On 13th March, 1936, Mr A.E. Purnell, the new station master of Kirkby Stephen addressed the annual dinner of LNER railwaymen at the Black Bull Hotel, Kirkby Stephen. He suggested to the 60 or so people present that the people of Kirkby Stephen seemed reluctant to travel by train 'these days' (the phrase 'rail shy' was used in the local press). He hoped there would be a big effort by the rail staff to encourage rail travel and make known 'the excellent facilities.'

In spite of this, it was suggested by Mr W. Herbert of Hartley Quarries that there might be a revival of trade in heavy industries which could increase the volume of traffic on the railways. However, the EVR was by this time, in effect, a passenger-carrying branch line with no significant freight traffic. If a future was to be assured there had to be a more concerted effort, especially from the top. The people of Kirkby Stephen, along with those in other towns along the line had not become rail-shy so much as bus-orientated.

There were other problems in addition to these posed by the competition of road transport. In the period 1920-22 there was a marked decrease over Stainmore in coke traffic (by some 50,000 tons), iron ore (by just over 4,000 tons) and road stone (some 18,000 tons). There was also a fall in the amount of livestock and general merchandise carried. Although there had been something of a return to post-war prosperity, the country was moving towards a recession. The General Strike of 1926 was soon to follow and the Great Depression was only just round the corner.

During World War I, the Government had taken control of the railways and in August 1921 the railways were handed back to the proprietors with payment being made to the companies at that point. This, however, was followed by the Act to bring about the amalgamation of the railways into four companies.

These developments in some sense blurred the financial problems some companies were facing. There was optimism that trade would pick up and the EVR, as part of the LNER in the 'big four' amalgamation, would see better times. At least one Director of the CK&PR was anxious for his company to become part of the LNER also, seeing its future prosperity linked with the east-west connection, rather than the LNWR-MR group.

Even so, the decline in trade resulted in the EVR being used less and less for through mineral workings. By 1928 these had dwindled to the point of being virtually non-existent. This is reflected in the fact that in that year, the curve from Eamont Bridge to Redhills went out of use. The east-west freight link was now by way of the former SD&LUR over to Tebay. However, the passenger traffic continued and special traffic also continued to use the line.

As mentioned earlier, a significant development occurred when a through train from Penrith to Darlington was introduced. This led to the line being inextricably bound up with the Stainmore line, and had considerable importance once moves were made to withdraw passenger services.

The line was also used as part of the route for some of the NER Circular Tours. In the timetable for 1899 there are no less than four circular tours in which the EVR is used in entirety or in part. Tour No. 1, starting and finishing in York, uses the whole of the branch, taking in Thirsk, Northallerton, Darlington, Durham, Newcastle, Hexham, Carlisle, Penrith, Keswick, Appleby, Barnard Castle and back to York. Penrith, Appleby and Kirkby Stephen are listed among the principal places of interest; in particular, the nine hole golf-course at Appleby.

Tour No. 10, starting and finishing at Newcastle, also includes the whole of the line, whilst Tours No. 6 (York to York) and 11 (Newcastle to Newcastle) take in the section from Kirkby Stephen to Appleby, returning thence by way of the Midland line to Hawes Junction.

In the middle years, the EVR had moments of mild drama and excitement. In the former category were the hold-ups and disruption caused by heavy snow falls, although quite often it was a consequence of the problems on Stainmore. In the latter category were those involving important visitors, one example being the visit, in September 1900, by the Duchess of York, to Sir Richard and Lady Musgrave at Eden Hall.

An interesting insight into the working conditions on the railway is given in an account of a presentation made in March 1936 when Mr John Cooper retired. John Cooper had spent nearly 50 years with the NER and later the LNER. For

The 10.00 am from Darlington arrives at Penrith on 13th June, 1957, headed by 'J21' class 0-6-0 No. 5103.
H.C. Casserley

'J21' class 0-6-0 No. 5028 with a valley train about to leave Penrith for Darlington in the early 1950s.
J.A. Peden

eight years of this period he was a porter at Warcop station and recounted how he had been required to work 14 hours a day, seven days a week. Once again there was a family involvement, John's father, Cuthbert Cooper, had also worked for the NER and had become a wagon inspector.

Although the early part of 20th century saw the EVR adopt a low profile, one factor which did give it a boost was the setting up, in the middle war years, of the Army Training Camp at Warcop. This resulted in personnel being brought in by rail, together with ammunition and heavy items of equipment such as tanks and lorries. A special unloading point was made at Warcop station to cater for these vehicles and it remained in use for a considerable period of years.

After World War II, in August 1945, a number of groups, representing various interests in the Lake District and Eden Valley, met to discuss the way in which transport links should be properly re-established. There were complaints, not about the railway services (which, it was suggested, few people now used), but about bus services. However, it was suggested that if the bus services could provide better connections at stations, there might be a greater use of train services. The main complaint, nevertheless, was that there were not enough vehicles to provide frequent services, and the buses were (possibly often dangerously) overcrowded as a result.

The day of the motor bus was about to reach something of a zenith; the competition it, in turn, had to try and meet from the private car had yet to come.

In spite of the complaints, Ribble Motor Services announced in August that a record number of passengers had been carried in the year up to 31st March.

At the same time, some improvements in the railway services were effected. Two extra trains were introduced each way on the CK&PR, and these gave some improved connections on the EVR.

In this post-war period, the towns and villages along the line were supplied with much of their coal requirements by the freight which travelled from Kirkby Stephen to Penrith each day. There were coal yards at most of the stations, until either they or their associated freight yards closed. Other commodities were brought in by this train and milk was taken out.

There were other users during this period.

Members of the Band of Hope used it from time to time to travel to Appleby where field-days were held. The groups used to march, with banners flying, from Appleby station to Broad Close. Boys from villages such as Winton who attended Appleby Grammar School would cycle to Musgrave to catch the train, joining those who had boarded at Kirkby Stephen. The carriages did not have corridor facilities and so a prefect was in charge in each one, keeping an eye on the behaviour of the pupils.

In the summer months the camping coaches at Kirkby Thore were a source of enjoyment for those using them as holiday bases.

However, during this period, it seems that the EVR continued to experience a further diminishing market. By the 1950s it was becoming clear that the future of the EVR, along with the line over Stainmore, was in some doubt. There was dissatisfaction by some users about old coaching stock, which was not in the best of condition, and stock that was increasingly difficult to keep properly clean.

All was not well.

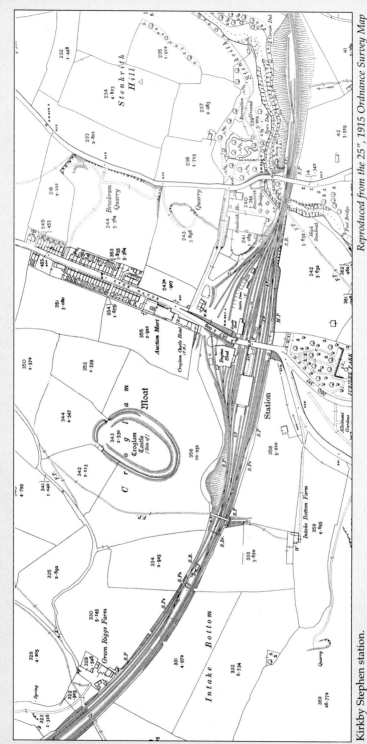

Kirkby Stephen station.

Reproduced from the 25", 1915 Ordnance Survey Map

Chapter Ten

Operational Procedures
and Motive Power

The line, as built, was essentially single track with some doubling on certain sections. Quite clearly there were hopes to double-track much of the line at a later date and provisions were made for this. However the need to carry out this work did not arise and so the aspirations of the planners were never realised.

As a result, operational procedures became those usually associated with working a single line, with the use of tablets and keys.

Arthur Watson, formerly a fireman on the branch, describes the procedure starting at Kirkby Stephen:

> You would start off at Kirkby Stephen West and get a disc tablet there. There were two tablets there, one for the Tebay line and one for the Penrith line. So that you didn't get mixed up, one had a square cut into the centre and the other had a triangle cut in the centre. They were also marked with the stations but you had to look at them closely when you picked the tablet up. It was in a loop to pick it up. The signalman at Kirkby Stephen West gave you that and then at Warcop you had it to change on the platform as you were moving. There you got a big heavy brass key which was in a pouch and on a ring. That took you to the crossing just past Appleby Station and there you gave that up and went onto double line. Then at Appleby West you picked up another tablet, a circular disc tablet, which took you to Kirkby Thore. You changed it there for another one which took you on to Clifton Moor. There was confusion sometimes because the two tablets at Kirkby Thore were very much alike and so you had to look very closely to make sure you hadn't forgotten to change them. At Clifton Moor you came onto double line again and so on to Penrith. Just past Clifton Moor there was the Eden Valley Junction and that was where you went onto the LMS main line.
>
> When you changed the tablet while you were moving, the fireman gave his up on a level with the engine number (on the cabside) and the signalman held his up higher. You had to hold your tablet fairly near the engine or the signalman was inclined to jump back and then he missed the tablet altogether so that you had to stop, walk back and get it!
>
> There is a story about an inspector driver and the Kirkby Thore tablets. This man was driving from Penrith one night and he forgot to change the tablet. He ended up at Appleby with the Clifton Moor tablet. It took him a long time to live it down but this sort of thing did happen from time to time. At stations where live were sidings, the tablet had to be slotted into a drawer by the point-handle on the ground frame. This had to be done to release the point and when any shunting was finished it was taken out and the token replaced in the pouch.

The original signalling equipment for the EVR was supplied by John Saxby, of Brighton. By the time the line was built, Saxby had been very much the pioneer in using boxes to replace the old style of signal platforms and so the line had boxes from the time it became operational. An interesting bill exists in connection with some work at Clifton Junction (the original south-facing junction). This is for a miscellany of equipment and the total monies involved is £156 17s. 10d. The opening statement reads 'Removing and refixing two

Kirkby Stephen East view looking towards Stainmore, 21st May, 1956.

P.B. Booth/N. Stead Collection

Kirkby Stephen East as seen from the road overbridge looking towards Penrith, 21st May, 1956.

P.B. Booth/N. Stead Collection

Above: Kirkby Stephen looking east into the station with the lines from Tebay and Penrith on the left, and the through mineral lines on the right, 16th November, 1959. *John Mallon*

Left: Kirkby Stephen Junction signal box *c.* 1965. *Adrian Vaughan Collection*

Below: Kirkby Stephen West Junction showing the Eden Valley Line converging on the left. A Central Division signal box (*centre*) has replaced the original Stockton & Darlington Railway one, which can be seen in the distance, whilst the World War II practice of replacing timber sleepers with a pair of concrete ones can be seen in the siding on the right. *John Mallon*

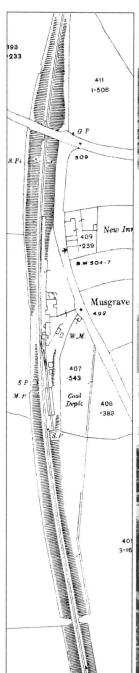

Above: Musgrave viaduct looking north.   *John Mallon*

Left: Musgrave station.   *Reproduced from the 25", 1915 Ordnance Survey Map*

Musgrave station looking north with the former goods yard and coal depot to the right. The mileages are measured from Kirkby Stephen.

John Mallon

Musgrave station looking south in LNER days.   *Eddie Foster*

Warcop station looking north *c.* 1960.   *Brunel University: Mowat/Locomotive Collection*

Warcop station.   *Reproduced from the 25", 1915 Ordnance Survey Map*

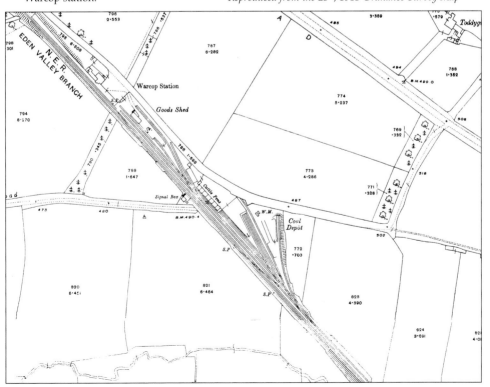

A late 1950s view of Warcop station looking south.

Warcop goods shed and goods yard looking south, 16th November, 1959.   *John Mallon*

Copeland viaduct looking north in November 1959. *John Mallon*

The junction of the Eden Valley line with the uncompleted connecting line to the Midland Railway on the left. *John Mallon*

Appleby *c.* 1905. The verandah has been enclosed and there is a goods line next to the passenger line. The southern exit to the single line is controlled by the original Appleby East signal box seen in the distance.   *L&GRP*

Appleby station looking north pre-1923 showing bracketed starting signals.   *L&GRP*

Railways at Appleby showing the proximity of the NER (*top*) and Midland Railway stations.

Reproduced from the 25", 1915 Ordnance Survey Map

Top: Appleby East goods yard *c*. 1950. A Ford type '7V' lorry stands by the side of the goods shed.
John Mallon Collection

Centre: The approach road to Appleby East in 1964. *H.C. Casserley*

Right: Appleby East signal box *c*. 1964. This box was originally called Appleby West, later becoming Appleby Station before becoming Appleby East. It stood at the north end of the station.
Adrian Vaughan Collection

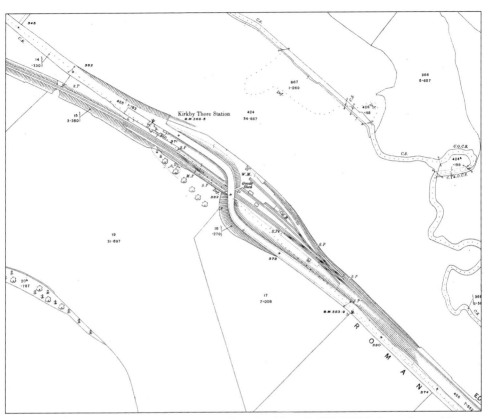

Kirkby Thore station. *Reproduced from the 25", 1915 Ordnance Survey Map*

Kirkby Thore looking west. This station was demolished during road improvements in the 1980s. *John Mallon*

Kirkby Thore goods yard and signal box in March 1953 looking towards Appleby.

North Road Museum

Temple Sowerby station.   *Reproduced from the 25", 1915 Ordnance Survey Map*

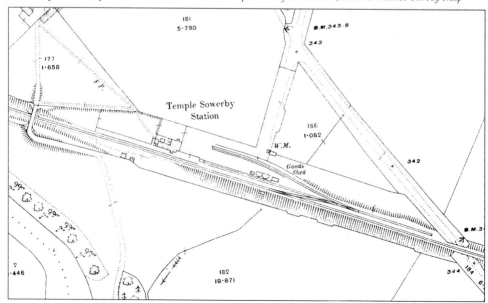

Temple Sowerby looking west in November 1959. All the station buildings on this line bore the date of construction above the entrance to the booking office. *John Mallon*

Skygarth viaduct looking north. *John Mallon*

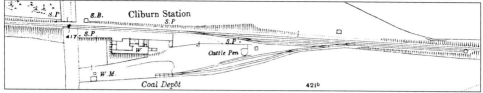

Cliburn station.

Reproduced from the 25", 1915 Ordnance Survey Map

Cliburn looking west, 17th November, 1959.

John Mallon

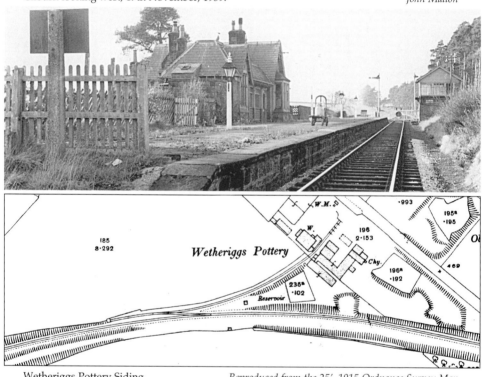

Wetheriggs Pottery Siding.

Reproduced from the 25', 1915 Ordnance Survey Map

Wetheriggs Pottery Siding looking east.

John Mallon

An early view of Clifton station. *Penrith Library*

A 1950s view of the station, by now known as Clifton Moor, looking towards Appleby.
N. Stead Collection

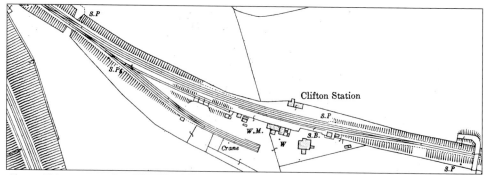

Above: Clifton station, the LNWR main line can be seen in the bottom left corner.

*Reproduced from the 25",
1915 Ordnance Survey Map*

Right: Clifton Moor station from the train in 1954.   *H.C. Casserley*

Below: Clifton Moor station looking north, November 1959.
John Mallon

Clifton Moor goods yard with the embankment of the LNWR main line from Euston to Carlisle on the left, 17th November, 1959. *John Mallon*

Eden Valley Junction looking north in November 1959. *John Mallon*

Clifton & Lowther signal box on the ex-LNWR main line in November 1959. The original south-facing junction of the Eden Valley Railway came through the trees beside the overbridge, and there was a turntable to the right.   *John Mallon*

The site of Eamont Junction looking north in 1959.   *John Mallon*

A view on Redhills curve in 1936.   *J.W. Armstrong Trust*

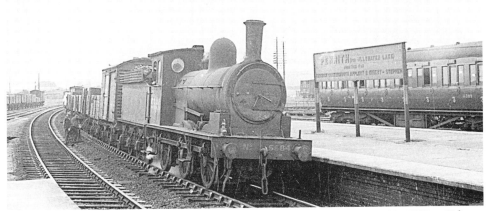

A goods train arrives at Penrith from the Eden Valley Line hauled by 'J25' 0-6-0 No. 5684 on 13th June, 1947. The engine had previously carried the number 2045 but had been re-numbered the previous August. *H.C. Casserley*

A pair of Ivatt 'Moguls' at Penrith station in August 1951. The train on the right is about to depart for the Eden Valley Line, the one on the left for Workington. *Real Photographs*

'J21' class 0-6-0 No. 65092 waits by No. 1 box at Penrith in April 1954 in readiness for a working on the Eden Valley Line.   *H.C. Casserley*

'J21' class 0-6-0 No. 65089 heads a train ready for departure from Penrith in May 1957.
                                                                                  Real Photographs

semaphore signals, altering wires and rods to six distant signals and connecting two pairs of points at Clifton Junction.' The word 'refixing' may be significant. It has been suggested that the company had been told to improve what was considered to be an inadequate system! It is possible the line had some interlocked boxes from the outset. Under the S&D additional boxes were built. When the branch became part of the NER, it was in the Central Division and this determined the style of later boxes. Tyer's No. 6 machines were used, probably with 'Absolute Block' between Clifton and the Eden Valley Junction.

Latterly, there were signal boxes for the branch at Kirkby Stephen West (renamed Kirkby Stephen Junction in 1948) Warcop, Appleby (Station - later renamed Appleby East) Appleby West (later renamed Appleby Junction) Kirkby Thore and Cliburn. The box at Kirkby Stephen West controlled access to the branch. It had a 50-lever Stevens frame. The box at Warcop (originally at the south side of the line but later replaced by another at the east end of the station platform) was NER Central Division Type C2a. It had a 15-lever Stevens frame. Appleby (Station) box was NER Central Division Type C1. It had a frame with 23 levers. This box controlled the level crossing adjacent to the station. (As mentioned earlier, this box was renamed Appleby East after Nationalisation. It had originally been named Appleby West. In 1909 it was renamed Appleby Station. After Nationalisation it became Appleby East, following the decision to name the ex-NER station at Appleby in this way; the ex-Midland station becoming Appleby West. Appleby East box was actually situated, as the original name suggests, to the west of Appleby East Station!) The other box, which had also at one stage been called Appleby West and which stood at the junction with the Midland line, was appropriately renamed after Nationalisation. The box at Kirkby Thore was used for the goods yard. Cliburn box was an NER non-standard type. It also controlled a level-crossing and contained a ground frame. Musgrave, Temple Sowerby and Clifton Moor stations each had a small 'hut' on the platform which acted as a signal cabin. Block posts were Kirkby Stephen West, Warcop, Appleby (Station) Appleby West, Kirkby Thore, Clifton Moor and Eden Valley Junction (West Coast Main Line). Temple Sowerby was reduced from a block post in 1908 and Cliburn in 1927. At Waitby there was a small brick hut with a ground frame for the level-crossing and one distant signal in each direction. There was also a keeper's cottage. There was a ground frame provided for the siding at Wetheriggs Pottery.

Motive Power and Rolling Stock

When reviewing the motive power used on the line, it is important to remember that although styled a branch line, it was, in reality, a through route. This resulted in a wide variety of motive power over the years, much of which would hardly be found on an ordinary branch line!

The Stockton and Darlington Railway was responsible for providing the first locomotives. The 4-4-0s of this company formed the early motive power. *Stag* is mentioned as one member of this type which frequently worked the line. The

'1001' class 0-6-0 No. 1184 at Kirkby Stephen in the early part of the present century. These locomotives hauled freight on the Eden Valley Line. *P. Strong Collection*

'1001' class 0-6-0 No. 1176 poses with its crew at Clifton station around the turn of the century. *Penrith Library*

freight was handled by the S&D class '1001' 0-6-0 locomotives. One of these No. 169 was named *Tufton*. Sadly, there is no 'Elliot' in the group.

When the NER assumed control of the line, together with the SD&LUR, Edward Fletcher was engineer. However, William Bouch (brother to Thomas) was engineer at Darlington and remained in charge there until 1875, when he retired. Fletcher, it seems, was happy with this arrangement although it has been suggested that he had very little say in it! The outcome was that Bouch's engines continued to dominate the line.

Latterly, he produced his class '238' 4-4-0s, a group of engines which were destined to numerous problems and eventually became known as 'Ginx's Babies'. The name 'Ginx' came from a fictional character invented by Edward Jenkins MP for a treatise on Poor Law reform. Ginx, distraught at the prospect of another child, vowed to drown it at birth. His attempts, however, failed. The '238s' were bedevilled by problems and in common parlance, these days, a 'ginx' (or jinx) is something which brings bad luck!

The 'Ginx's Babies', in a rebuilt form, appeared on the branch in the 1890s working passenger trains. During the last part of the 19th century, more and more of Fletcher's locomotives made an appearance.

These included the class '398' 0-6-0 type first built at Gateshead in 1872, the class '901' 2-4-0, also built originally in 1872, the Bogie Tank Passenger 0-4-4 which came out in 1874 and class '1440,' Fletcher's last design before his retirement in 1883. The '1440' was a small wheel version of his '901'.

The class '398' was designed for freight traffic and weighed, including tender, 66¼ tons. Fletcher had a policy of using the standard NER livery for all engines and so these freight locomotives appeared in the attractive green and fully lined out.

The class '901' was built for express passenger service and came to work on the branch in mid-1880s. These locomotives with 7 ft driving wheels had given excellent service on the main lines before enjoying the idyllic charms of the Eden Valley.

The Bogie Tank Passenger (BTP) locomotives had driving wheels of 5 ft diameter and also had the full treatment as far as livery was concerned. They must have looked a fine sight as they carried out passenger workings on the branch. This class became 'G6' at the grouping.

The class '1440' also appeared on the branch. These, like the class '901', had a 2-4-0 wheel arrangement but had driving wheels of 6 ft diameter. By all accounts they were very sound engines.

Edward Fletcher was succeeded by Alexander McDonnell who had only a brief stay with the NER. His reforms proved unpalatable and, after only one year, he found the opposition too much and resigned. His class '38' 4-4-0 engines, although tried on the line, did not prove a match for the '901s', although there may have been problems with a lot of prejudice, McDonnell was so unpopular.

After McDonnell's somewhat hasty departure, Henry Tennant, the General Manager, stepped into the breach until Thomas Worsdell was appointed in 1885. After Thomas, came Wilson, his younger brother, and the latter, who succeeded him in 1890, stayed until 1910, when Vincent Raven took over.

'D3' class 4-4-0 No. 4077, a Penrith engine, at Kirkby Stephen on a Penrith-Darlington working on 7th June, 1935.

H.C. Casserley

The Penrith 'E4', No. 7408 at Kirkby Stephen.

During the period from Tennant to Raven, a number of classes were produced which eventually found their way onto the branch.

The class 'O', designed by Wilson Worsdell, was operating local passenger trains by the end of the 1920s. This class of tank engines, with a wheel arrangement of 0-4-4, became 'G5' at the grouping. A photograph exists showing No. 2089 at Penrith. This locomotive, renumbered 7318 in 1948 and later 67318, was a Stockton engine. The class 'B' and 'B1', 0-6-2Ts, designed by Thomas Worsdell were also used on the line. These became 'N8s'.

The Tennant class '1463' was another type which appeared on the line. Records indicate that the class '901' and the Tennants were eventually replaced by T.W. Worsdell's 'D23' class 4-4-0s (Ex-NER 'G' class) and these appeared in the early 1930s. The 'D23s' gave way to the ex-Great Northern Railway Ivatt 'D3' class 4-4-0s. As far as the Darlington engines were concerned, the daily roster for the 'D3s' might well include a trip from Darlington to Penrith and back to Darlington followed by a Darlington to Kirkby Stephen turn and then back to Darlington.

An interesting class of engines put to work on the line was the 'E4'. These engines were designed by J. Holden of the GER and were used for hauling passenger trains. They were brought in to replace the 'D3s'. The closing of the Redhills curve, which it will be recalled facilitated transfer from the EVR to the CK&PR without reversing in Penrith, resulted in such a reversal becoming necessary again. The turntable at Penrith, however, could only accommodate locomotives up to 42 ft in length and the 'D3s' were 42 ft 10 in.! As a result, these engines had to travel considerable distances tender first and this was deemed unsatisfactory. The 'E4s' were the only four-coupled engines available at the time that could be turned at Penrith.

Perhaps the locomotives most fondly remembered in connection with the line were the seemingly ubiquitous 'J' classes. In particular, the group which eventually became the 'J21s' (formerly 'C' and 'C1') designed by Thomas Worsdell, and his brother Wilson's 'P1s' which became the 'J25s'.

The 'J21s' were first built in 1886; the 'J25s' in 1898. These classes did sterling work on the line, hauling both freight and passenger trains.

It was, in fact, the 'J21s' and 'J25s' which were the 'survivors' as far as the NER locomotives were concerned, remaining, as they did, well into the period after Nationalisation. They were eventually joined by H.A. Ivatt's '2MT' 2-6-0 and '4MT' 2-6-0 classes which were introduced in 1946 and 1947. These were followed by the Standard classes; class '2' 2-6-0, class '4' 2-6-0 and class '3' 2-6-2T tank engines. In the last of these groups Nos. 82027, 82028 and 82029 worked the branch. It seems the engine crews particularly welcomed the Standard class '2s' after the Ivatt locomotives because the latter were felt to be badly designed and uncomfortable from the crew's point of view. The Standard '2s' seemed luxury in comparison! Standard class '3' 2-6-0 No. 77003 and Standard class '4' 2-6-0, No. 76049 would have a particularly onerous task later in the story.

Inevitably, steam started to give way to diesel. In 1958 dmus took over the Penrith to Darlington passenger workings. A great deal of publicity was attached to this particular transition. Notices appeared in the Press advertising the introduction of a faster service and the timetable made the point that the

In 1952 the local passenger trains were in the hands of Ivatt class '2s'. Here No. 46481 is about to leave Penrith with the 10.30 am to Kirkby Stephen. *R.H. Fullagar/N. Stead Collection*

'J21' class 0-6-0 No. 65092 on the turntable at Penrith in April 1954. *H.C. Casserley*

An Ivatt class '4' 2-6-0 heads a goods train near New Hall, between Appleby and Warcop. *Peter Walton Collection*

service was operated by diesel trains. However, in spite of this promising step, the service was soon under threat. In the 1970s and 1980s diesel classes '31', '40' and '47' made visits to the line, especially in connection with the movement of troops and equipment to and from the Army Training Centre at Warcop. Although the general view seems to be that the last visit was in 1989, there is one reported sighting of a class '47' as late as 1990.

In addition to the regular motive power, this line, rather like the Ingleton branch, just to the south, was visited by a legion of different locomotive classes when it was used either by specials or when the line acted as a relief route for the West Coast or Settle & Carlisle lines. Any of the types of motive power using these routes might be found on the EVR. A considerable amount of anecdotal evidence exists and this includes accounts of visits by a wide variety of LMS locomotives such as 'Jubilees', 'Patriots', Stanier '8Fs' and '5MTs'.

After Nationalisation Kirkby Stephen Shed was designated 51H, as a member of the Darlington sub-group. In 1958, following regional reorganisation, the shed was placed in the Midland Region, Kirkby Stephen being, in effect, the divide, with the Midland to the West and the Eastern Region to the East and, as a member of the Carlisle sub-group, became 12E. Within weeks, this was revised to 12D. The last shedmaster under the Eastern Region was William Sanderson and the first under the Midland Region was Gordon Leslie Carr. The former, it seems, was a very amicable and well liked man but the latter, who stayed for only 18 months, was seen by many of the workforce as a hard task-master and a keen disciplinarian. He was not popular; but, then again, he had come from the Midland!

About a dozen locomotives were shedded at any one time at Kirkby Stephen in LNER days with some of the branch workings drawn from these. Under BR, this number did not change significantly. In 1951 there were eleven locomotives shedded at Kirkby Stephen. These consisted of six 'J21s' (Nos. 65028, 65040, 65047, 65089, 65100 and 65103) together with five 'J25s' (Nos. 65653, 65655, 65673, and 65695). Two years later, there was a mix of Midland and Eastern engines with Ivatt '2MT' 2-6-0s, Nos. 46471, 46474, 46477,46478, 46480 joining 65047, 65655, 65673 and 65695. By 1960, all the 'J' class engines had gone, as had all but one of Ivatt's engines, No. 46470. There were still 11 engines but the other 10 were Standard classes. These consisted of six class '4' 2-6-0s (Nos. 76020, 76022, 76023, 76047, 76051 and 76052) with four class '2' 2-6-0s (Nos. 78013, 78017, 78018 and 78019). Eventually, these locomotives were transferred to Carlisle.

The NER had shedding facilities at Penrith. This shed was opened in 1865 by the LNWR. After some protracted negotiations which also involved the CK&PR, its use by the NER was agreed in 1873. In the early 1920s a '901' class was stabled there and later a Tennant 2-4-0. There was also at one time 'G5' No. 1016 and this worked all the daily return journeys between its home base and Kirkby Stephen. Later a 'D3' arrived. This was No. 4077 and it remained at Penrith for about a year, during the period 1935-36. When the 'E4' class appeared one of these was kept at Penrith. First came No. 7308 and then, as a replacement, No. 7411. No. 7416 which took the place of 7411 was the last engine to be shedded at Penrith because in the late 1930s the shedding facilities were relinquished, although it seems that in any case, latterly, they had only been used to house the last working of the day in readiness for the following morning. However, locomotives for the line continued to use water and coaling facilities.

As far as rolling stock is concerned, the vast majority of the items were, of course mineral wagons. In the heyday of freight these mineral wagons were used for the transportation of coal, coke, iron ore, pig-iron and lime but as the branch gradually lost its significance as a through route for freight, the local goods comprised a small miscellany of wagons. Coal for local use still formed an important part of this, with milk wagons (there was an Express Dairy depot at Appleby) fruit and fish being included as well. Even some of the smaller businesses found it worthwhile to have their own wagons. J.J. Bousefield, for example, owned just two.

The wagons were operated loose coupled and automatic brakes were a rarity. One notable exception to this was the fruit vans. Mention has been made of the dairy at Appleby. One crew-man recalls the practice of the early passenger train from Darlington to Penrith picking up a milk wagon at Barnard Castle for delivery to Appleby. It seems this additional 32 tons made the difference between an easy run and 'having to flog the engine to death'. A number of small businesses in the Eden Valley, apart from the quarries, found the line vital for trade. Tommy Longstaff made, it is said, the largest number of hay rakes in the country and sent them to a wide variety of destinations. These, together with the hay racks, carts and wheelbarrows, which he made at Warcop around the turn of the century, could fill a siding full of wagons at Warcop every two months, ready for dispatch. Not only that; the trees for the timber he used came in by rail, as well. Warcop, with all the activity, was by far the busiest place on the line.

The coaching stock used on the branch was of the vestibule type although composite stock, which it appears had been condemned for main line use for reasons such as poor heating systems or gas lighting, eventually found its way onto the branch. In the early 1960s there were frequent complaints about the poor state and cleanliness of the coaching stock.

Some Operating Incidents

During World War II standards on the branch, in common with other places, fell noticeably. This, it seems, was reflected in the problems associated with maintaining equipment at a reasonable level and, possibly related to this, the matter of morale. Breaches in regulations often went without action or even comment because, it is suggested, there were manpower problems.

An incident cited as an example of this involved a class 'J21' (No. 1575). After leaving Appleby, the Westinghouse brake pump had stopped. It leaked so much that the brake was completely ineffective and when the train reached the bottom of Kirkby Thore bank it went straight over the crossover and became derailed. A nasty experience for the Darlington crew in charge! This event occurred in 1942.

There are numerous tales told which reflect the day to day practices in the post-war years. There were always problems with cattle on the line and it seems, for a variety of reasons, farmers and railwaymen had to share the blame for the accidents which happened. Leaving gates open was an obvious and common problem although it seems there was a practice, latterly, of freight crews rescheduling their timings to suit other commitments! One situation described involved the decision to attend a funeral at a certain time which would not have been possible by keeping to the scheduled working. These changes were always agreed at a 'local' level but could result, of course, in a freight turning up when a farmer did not expect it, so risking havoc!

On one occasion a farmer who lived between Appleby and Kirkby Thore and who had to take his herd across the line to grazing land, opened the gates to allow animals to cross back to the farm. The dog had gone over the line to send the cattle back, when the early morning pick-up goods appeared. Before the farmer could close the gate the dog had driven the cows into the side of the train. The engine was coasting and all the wagons were buffered up. The driver, Bill Proudlock, was powerless to do anything. One of the unfortunate animals was caught under the train and rolled over and over until it reached an empty wagon. This wagon was lifted high into the air and thrown into the adjoining field. It actually landed the right way up!

There were other similar incidents with cattle killed or maimed so badly that they had to be destroyed.

Then there was the practice of allowing firemen and others to 'have a go' at driving the locomotive. This usually passed unnoticed and without incident. However, on one occasion, it certainly did not. Passed fireman Cecil Brayshaw, together with an engine cleaner, took charge of Standard class '2' No. 78019. which was working tender first. They set out from Appleby for Warcop with a permanent way living van. The cleaner was driving. At Warcop they failed to observe the home signal was against them and without stopping careered through the crossover and collided with No. 78017. The two engines met tender to tender and the water tank of No. 78017 was severed completely from its chassis. No. 78019, which has since been preserved, still has a distorted drag box! The passed fireman, incidentally, received a severe reprimand.

The line saw no major incidents as far as accidents were concerned but there were a few fatalities, usually the result of people not taking care when walking along the track. The death of the cloth salesman from Carlisle has already been mentioned. Another unfortunate incident involved three platelayers who were walking on the actual track between Musgrave and Warcop. In this accident, which occurred in 1943, Anthony Kirkbride, who was walking in the centre, was knocked down and killed by a train. The others, who were walking on the outer parts of the sleepers, either side, were simply flung aside and, fortunately, were not seriously hurt. The whole business was very traumatic for the driver of the locomotive, Fred Wilson. As mentioned previously, in such a small concern many of the workforce knew each other well.

There are other situations which, whilst not particularly amusing at the time, have a mildly humorous ring when viewed in retrospect. Kirkby Thore station was at the bottom of a dip. The continual climbing and heavy braking of trains caused the rails to creep down gradually, eventually closing up the end clearance. The remedy was to cut out four and a half inches at the lowest point, drill one fresh hole in each rail for the fish-plate and wedge the joints open for a considerable distance until the four and a half inch gap could be closed. Somehow, on one occasion when the work was to be carried out on two consecutive Sundays, the instructions were misunderstood and, in addition, two different gangs were to do the work. On the second Sunday the second gang started at the 'wrong end' with the result that they ended up wedging over two and a half miles of track. At this stage it was getting dark and so they were only able to retrieve some of the spent wedges. It is reported that the morning goods 'found' the rest, much to the discomfort of the crew!

There are tales too of the 'cloots' (sponge cloths) issued to the firemen; one each day for use when handling the fire irons or as towels and how the platelayers tried to beg these much prized items and would sometimes raid the stores to get at them. One young new trainee fireman happened on one occasion to drop his cloot over the side whilst an engine was shunting at Warcop. So anxious was he to recover it that he immediately jumped off the footplate while the engine was moving. As he was climbing back on board he failed to notice that the engine was approaching one of the docks and he was crushed between the two. Fortunately his injuries were not fatal.

In many ways the pace of life on the railway in these post-war years and into the early 1960s seems to have been steady and very pleasant; indeed many would insist, enjoyable. However there were dark clouds beginning to gather on the horizon. Some would say there was apathy and neglect in high and possibly not so high places. Others would argue that circumstances had changed radically. No doubt there is some truth in both. What is for sure is that by the end of the 1950s the EVR was heading for a critical stage in its history.

LMS and BR Standard types have ousted the NER engines in this May 1956 view of Kirkby Stephen Shed.   *P.B. Booth/N. Stead Collection*

Chapter Eleven

The Fight for Survival (1952-1962)

During the 1950s and 1960s it became clear that a radical review of Britain's rail network was needed. Once World War II was over and engineering expertise could be vigorously applied to civilian enterprise, the development of the internal combustion engine moved rapidly and road transport, private and commercial, began to erode the influence of the railways.

The once-handling principle used in road transport, instead of the twice-loading procedure often needed when goods travel by rail, is a marked advantage. Although the railways eventually embraced the internal combustion engine and a once-loading principle came nearer with the freightliner approach, it was not before the motor car and commercial vehicle had dramatically altered the way people and goods were moved. As a result, what started as a steady trickle of change in what has now become known as 'rationalisation' soon gave way to a torrent, as Beeching's proposals in 1963 and after were put into effect.

Because the EVR was virtually inextricably linked with the Stainmore route, not least once the Penrith-Darlington service was introduced, the proposal to close the line was tied up with the wider issue of closing the Stainmore line. In spite of this, the main opposition to closure appears to have come from the Eden Valley and the fight is referred to frequently as one to save 'the Eden Valley Line'.

There is an impression that a move by British Railways to effect closure seemed to take some by surprise, but there had been a gradual erosion of the facilities over quite a long period of time.

Musgrave was the first station to be affected; this was closed completely on 3rd November, 1952. A year later, on 7th December, 1953, Kirkby Thore was also closed completely and, on the same day, Temple Sowerby was closed to passengers, although a goods facility was retained.

There was now a lull in the process. It was almost three years later, on 17th September, 1956, that Cliburn was closed to all traffic.

This meant that by the beginning of 1957 only three stations remained fully operational: Clifton, Appleby and Warcop. By now it should have been evident that the writing was on the wall.

A note at the bottom of the timetable for 1958 furnishes the information that services have been withdrawn from Cliburn, Kirkby Thore and Temple Sowerby. Further, that the locality is served by omnibuses of Ribble Motor Services Ltd from Penrith or Appleby. The bus was taking over!

Any fear about BR intentions, however, might well have been allayed for many in February 1958, when the introduction of a 'faster diesel service' between Penrith and Darlington was announced. There were three trains each way every day, with an additional service on the EVR between Appleby and Penrith. This left Penrith at 12.55 pm, arrived in Appleby at 1.19, left at 1.27 and arrived back in Penrith at 1.50 pm. There was also an additional service

'J21' class 0-6-0 No. 65092 ready to depart with the 10.30 am Penrith to Darlington train on 26th April, 1954. *H.C. Casserley*

The same train is seen at Appleby East on 26th April, 1954. *H.C. Casserley*

between Kirkby Stephen and Darlington.

In spite of this apparent demonstration of support by BR for keeping the line open, Mr W.M.F. Vane, MP for Westmorland, felt it necessary to express his concern during a debate in the House of Commons on Tuesday 25th February, involving a BTC Bill. In view of what appeared to him to be a number of uncertainties, he held the view that a conference should be held to discuss the whole business of transport in the Lake District. He expressed the wish that BR would be more co-operative over branch lines in the area. He advocated more publicity for railway facilities, including wider advertising. He even went as far as to plead a case for the use of hardwood instead of softwood sleepers (later, BR was to use concrete sleepers on the branch!), because hardwood could be obtained from home sources.

The Joint Parliamentary Secretary to the Ministry of Transport thanked Mr Vane for his observations and assured him the BTC would take note of them (including home-grown hardwood).

A number of suggestions followed Mr Vane's remarks. One was that a new railbus being tried out by BR might be introduced, to give greater economy. At 11 tons, with a 150 hp engine, and travelling up to 55 mph, it could take 46 passengers, possibly a realistic capacity for the line.

There the matter seemed to rest, but only a few months later, in September, services were cut. The North Westmorland Rural Council complained about this move, only to be told, in a written reply read out at the meeting on Saturday 13th September:

> BTC express reluctance but insist they must operate on an economic basis. The services latterly have proved to be uneconomic.

The railway was not alone in facing problems of this sort. As it happened, in February, the General Manager of the Ribble Bus Company admitted that more than half the services in the rural areas were running at a loss and some might have to be abandoned.

Two years later, in May 1959, only three years before the railway was to celebrate its centenary, rumours which had been circulating about possible proposals to close the line came nearer to reality when a number of steps were taken which seemed to indicate British Railways' intentions.

It was announced that the rail services in the area which included the EVR were 'under review'. The lines involved included the EVR, the CK&PR and the old SD&LUR over to Tebay.

BR at Barrow issued a statement on Wednesday 6th May, which was reported in the *Cumberland and Westmorland Herald*:

> We can only say that all services and indeed all stations throughout the region are under review. The explanation is to be found in the present financial position of the railways and the statutory obligation placed upon us to pay our way.

The statement goes on to deny that there are any proposals to close the CK&PR but, as the writer of the report points out, no such denial is made about the EVR.

FASTER DIESEL SERVICE

Darlington -- Barnard Castle -- Penrith

(and Intermediate Stations)

WEEKDAYS until further notice

	a.m.	a.m.	p.m.	p.m.	SX p.m.	SO p.m.
Darlington dep.	6-23	10-48	—	4-34	10-34	11- 0
Barnard Castle arr. ...	6-56	11-24	—	5-11	11- 7	11-33
Barnard Castle dep. ...	7- 1	11-26	—	5-13	11- 9	11-35
		p.m.				
Kirkby Stephen arr. ...	7-40	12- 5	—	5-52	11-48	12-14
Kirkby Stephen dep. ..	7-42	12- 7	—	5-54	——	——
Warcop dep.	7-51	12-16	—	6- 3	——	——
Appleby East dep. ...	7-58	12-23	1-27	6-10	——	——
Clifton Moor dep.	8-14	12-39	1-42	6-26	——	——
Penrith arr.	8-22	12-47	1-50	6-34	——	——

SX—Saturdays Excepted.

SO—Saturdays Only.

	a.m.	a.m.	p.m.	p.m.	p.m.
Penrith dep.	—	10-12	12-55	3-20	8-35
Clifton Moor dep.	—	10-20	1 -3	3-28	8-43
Appleby East dep.	—	10-36	1-19	3-44	8-59
Warcop dep.	—	10-45	—	3-53	9- 8
Kirkby Stephen arr. ...	—	10-55	—	4- 3	9-18
Kirkby Stephen dep. ..	7-15	10-57	—	4- 5	9-20
Barnard Castle arr. ...	7-53	11-35	—	4-43	9-58
Barnard Castle dep. ...	8- 2	11-37	—	4-45	10- 5
		p.m.			
Darlington arr.	8-35	12-10	—	5-19	10-38

Ask for folder giving full details of this service.

(BRITISH RAILWAYS)   (102217)

An advert for 'Faster Diesel Services' in February 1958.

On Monday 4th May, a meeting was held at Kirkby Stephen at which BR officials met the representatives of various departments. This followed previous discussions between railway management and rail unions.

The message put over was that the EVR would almost certainly close by the end of the year. For some, the news that passenger services might be withdrawn was not altogether unexpected. It was a well known fact that passenger traffic was small.

In July 1959, when the battle to save the line was gathering pace, a survey was carried out which revealed that during the course of a week 27 passengers left Barnard Castle in one day (travelling on three trains) and 56 people left the trains at Penrith. Only one station on the line, Kirkby Stephen, had reached double figures with people getting on and off.

Further, that on a summer Saturday 120 passengers left Barnard Castle in three trains and 123 got off at Penrith. It was alleged that in a survey carried out during the winter only 20 people left Barnard Castle in three trains on a certain weekday, and 30 on a Saturday.

These, however, were figures produced for the British Transport Commission and it hardly goes without saying they were a matter for dispute when produced as evidence.

During the course of 1959 there was a growing feeling that in spite of the silence the situation was far from dormant, and that closure of the EVR would sooner or later be proposed. In view of this Appleby Council declared that it was prepared to fight such a proposal when (rather than if) it arose.

Yet there were still occasions when any idea of closure (as opposed to withdrawing passenger services) was virtually denied. On Saturday 28th November at a Conservative supper club gathering at the Pennine Hotel at Kirkby Stephen, W.M.F. Vane, MP for Westmorland, spoke in reply to questions about the future of the railways in the area. The conference which he had hoped for had not taken place, and although he was realistic in his views about the poor use of the railways and the decline in passenger traffic, when drawn on the EVR in particular he said that the railway had been built as a mineral line, and that was where he felt its future might be.

If the people present found any reassurance in this, their hopes that BR had any intention of retaining the line were short-lived.

At a meeting of the Transport Users' Consultative Committee (TUCC) for the North Eastern Area held at Darlington on Wednesday 9th December (1959), BR announced it proposed to withdraw the Barnard Castle to Penrith passenger service and to close sections of the line. The decision, the meeting was informed, had been made on the grounds of economy.

Further, BR made it clear that it proposed to take up the track on the whole of the EVR with the exception of the section between Appleby and Hartley Quarries (a mile beyond Kirkby Stephen). The section would be retained to make it possible for freight traffic to link with the Midland at Appleby.

It was pointed out by the chairman that part of the line (including the EVR) from Darlington came within the remit of the TUCC for the North West, who would therefore have a voice.

The 28 local authorities in the area served by the line together with other

A dmu leaving Appleby East for Penrith. This was operating the much publicised 'fast diesel service'. *N. Stead Collection*

A dmu stands at Appleby East *c.* 1960. *Brunel University: Mowat/Locomotive Collection*

interested parties would be notified. Any objections would need to be lodged before 23rd January, 1960.

One of the proposals involved diverting through traffic via Newcastle-upon-Tyne and Carlisle.

A committee was formed to deal with objections, the chairman of this being Alderman J. Gray of Whitley Bay. It was recognised that this committee would need to work closely with a similar committee from the North Western area.

Appleby Borough Council, already anticipating this move, decided to engage Mr K.B. Edwards, a barrister, to represent them at any public inquiry about the future of the EVR.

The writer of the editorial in the *Cumberland and Westmorland Herald* of 12th December noted:

> The last date for objections is 23rd January, a very short period when the Christmas and New Year holidays intervene. There are 28 local authorities in the area covered by the Penrith-Barnard Castle line and that does not give much time for these authorities to convene meetings.

There followed a rebuke for the Penrith Urban Council for failing to appreciate the urgency of the situation.

When the battle begins, 'British Railways artillery will be in full blast . . . those in opposition will have to be prepared with something more effective than pop-guns.'

In July of that year, the Penrith Urban Council had agreed 'not to associate themselves with any proposal for engaging counsel to represent the authorities concerned in any enquiry or proceedings.'

At a meeting in November they had 'decided to await further information before taking any action on a suggestion that they should join with the Appleby Council in engaging a barrister.'

Possibly smarting from the rebuke of the editorial, the Council, at a meeting on Wednesday 16th December, decided they would, after all, join Appleby Borough Council in opposing the plans to close the EVR. The members agreed to share the cost of engaging the barrister to represent them at an inquiry.

The members were keen to stress that they had not been apathetic towards closure, they had just been watching the situation closely.

It was pointed out during this meeting that passenger trains on the branch did not run at convenient times for many people. Trains left Kirkby Stephen at 7.42 am, 12.02 pm, and 5.54 pm. No attempt had been made by BR to adjust the timings to meet local needs. Whilst the introduction of diesel units was welcomed, fares had increased, making travelling by rail unpopular. Why, wondered the chairman, if the 7.42 am from Kirkby Stephen had to stand in Penrith station for two hours doing nothing, should it not run back to Kirkby Stephen and return to Penrith at 9.30 am, as this would be more convenient for a lot of people. In the same way, the 12.02 pm stood at Penrith for two hours and a similar principle could be applied. The train journey from Kirkby Stephen to Penrith lasted 42 minutes; the journey by bus was two hours! There seemed to be a feeling that British Railways had not made any real effort to make the line viable.

On Saturday 2nd January, 1960 North Westmorland Council (NWC) held a meeting. The members of this Council, too, decided to join the fight against the closure of the EVR, and help to finance the barrister. The members of the NWC felt strongly that the Transport Commission had very much overstated its case by exaggeration and over-emphasis.

One disappointment however, to those opposing closure, was that the Lake District Planning Board decided not to join the fight and take action against the BR proposals. At a meeting on 5th January, 1960 the closure was discussed and the members had a copy of a protest from Penrith Urban Council to the Transport Commission.

Sir Percy Hope, who was present at the meeting, expressed surprise. He felt the area would be disadvantaged by the loss of the railway and moved an amendment to the resolution that 'no action should be taken'. After some debate and following a vote, the amendment was lost; the Lake District Planning Board remained silent on the issue.

Meetings in the area involving local politicians could not take place, it seemed, without the EVR proposals being aired. Mr William Whitelaw (as he was then), MP for Penrith and the Border, speaking at the Penrith Rotary Club at the George Hotel, Penrith, on Monday 4th January on the theme 'Outlook for 1960', touched on it in discussing transport in the district. He commented:

Locally we have the line from Penrith to Keswick (the CK&PR), the gateway to the northern end of the Lake District. I should have thought it would be a disastrous mistake to close that gateway. (As to the Penrith-Barnard Castle line:) It is a means of access to the Lake District from the North East coast and the only thing that could be done was for the local authorities and everyone in the area to present the strongest possible case to put before the TUCC. There is a school of thought which says that committee is merely a rubber stamp which always does what British Railways want, but I am assured that is not so.

Plans for opposing the closure now moved ahead rapidly. The three main groups from the area opposing the closure, the Appleby Borough Council, Penrith Council and North Westmorland Rural Council, drew up battle plans at a joint meeting held in Penrith Town Hall on Thursday 14th January.

The chair was taken by Mr G. Johnston and a total of seven members representing these three councils met with the barrister to discuss the closure proposals. There was also a representative present at the meeting from Westmorland County Council.

The outcome of this meeting was an impressive fifteen-point statement giving the grounds for the objection. In this, it was argued that transport users in their areas would suffer undue hardship, inconvenience and financial loss, if the BTC proposal were put into effect.

The statement points out that the lines which it proposed should be closed provide the only two direct links between the industrial area of Durham and Teesside, and the industrial areas of West Cumberland and the Lake District. The argument continues by making it clear that these lines are not branch lines 'serving only a prosperous agricultural valley or traversing bare Pennine country but important cross-country communications linking East and West strategically, economically and industrially.'

Further it is argued that the BTC case is flawed in some of its statistical information. Population figures, for example, quoted by the BTC are below the actual ones; the Commission reckons that only 6,500 persons in the Penrith Rural District will be affected by the proposal, when a more realistic figure is 40,290. This area, in particular, involves the EVR.

Other issues involve the slow and inconvenient nature of bus services (for example, it would not be possible to make a return journey from Appleby to Darlington in the same day), old age pensioners would have to walk miles to draw their pensions, relatives and friends would find it difficult to visit patients in hospital in Carlisle, holiday traffic would be adversely affected, newspapers would not be received in the Eden Valley on the morning of the day of publication, mail would be delayed, fish from Hull and Grimsby would arrive unfit for human consumption, livestock transported out of the area would suffer as a result of longer journeys.

In addition, the diverting of freight via Newcastle and Carlisle would almost certainly give rise to delays, resulting in loss, frustration and complaint. The result would be more freight forced on to the already busy roads.

The document goes on to question the validity of the statement regarding the financial situation in relation to the EVR. Important omissions have been made regarding the forwarded and received merchandise, limestone minerals and livestock at Kirkby Stephen and Appleby East. This impairs what, in the opposition view, is a clear financial picture. In addition to this, in Statement 1 of the BTC memorandum relating to the closure proposal, a net estimated saving of £103,274 is envisaged. The Council Statement suggests that as the figures are based, presumably, on those for 1958, and there has been a marked upturn in the economy, especially in relation to heavy industry, the figures are misleading, not least because the North-East, as an area of such industry, stands to see improvements.

This is supported by the fact that in the final quarter of 1959, crude steel output was some 30 per cent higher than in the previous year. In the first three weeks of December 1959, ingot steel production was the highest ever recorded in the UK, and a large rise was forecast for 1960.

Link this with the fact that limestone is forwarded from Kirkby Stephen and Warcop to the steel-making areas of the North-East, and the rise in production had led to a greater demand, it becomes apparent that the BTC argument is not based on a realistic appraisal of the situation.

Further, high tonnages of coke and coal have been dispatched from Durham to Barrow and Millom. In view of all this, it is argued that:

(i) the said lines are now paying their way, or will pay their way by August 1960.

(ii) an annual increase in net income of £103,274 or an annual reduction of £103,274 in net loss is now being effected or will be achieved by August 1960.

Item 13 in the Council Submission repeats much of what has already been said, but pleads a case for optimism in view of the upturn in the economy. There is an exhortation at the end of the document to attract additional freight, speed up services and canvass services by employing an agent.

So the case was prepared. On the face of it, the approach by the councils seems positive and optimistic; this contrasts sharply with British Railways' stance.

The considerable amount of effort that had gone into making a case against closure was put to good effect. At a meeting of the NW and NE TUCC, held at Carlisle on Wednesday 24th February, objections were heard from a wide variety of persons and institutions; 51 in all. They included Members of Parliament, local authorities, industrial concerns and private individuals.

The MPs present were H.J. Boyden, W.M.F. Vane and T. Kitson. The local authorities included Cumberland, Durham and Westmorland. The group of local councils that had been involved in the preparation of the detailed case, outlined previously, were also well to the fore, together with a number of others.

Industrial concerns included Sir Hedworth Williamson's Limeworks Ltd, Hartley Quarries, Dorman Long (Steel) Ltd from Middlesbrough and, in the west, Millom Haematite Ore and Iron Company Limited.

On another front, the British Hotels and Restaurants Association, together with the Lake District Hotels and Caterers Association were represented, along with a number of Trades of Commerce Groups. The Westmorland Labour Party, the Ramblers' Association and the YHA were also out in force.

Add to these the private individuals, and there was assembled a body of objectors representing many groups from a wide spectrum which would be affected by the closure. It was reckoned that never before in the North of England had there been such an event!

British Railways' case was presented by Mr C.A. Haygreen from the headquarters of the North Eastern Region, York, who also represented London Midland Region, Euston. He opened by setting aside possible arguments about whether the line should be run as a public service with acceptable losses, or whether it should be a profit-making business. His brief was concerned with the latter, and British Railways felt they would, in the light of that, be better off without the line.

He argued that:

(i) the passenger service was losing £10,000 each year;

(ii) freight, most of which was 'through freight', was also running at a loss.

In view of these factors, through freight could be diverted, so saving some £53,000 a year; an additional £50,000 would be saved by withdrawing passenger services. The arguments for making these savings and effecting closure included the double-heading needed on the Stainmore route, against one engine moving a larger load on an alternative route (two locomotives with 22 wagons, against one locomotive with 34 wagons, were the figures quoted); the closing of Kirkby Stephen motive power depot and the fact that (and this seems to be begging the question) removal of freight would result in the passenger traffic becoming unacceptably uneconomic.

Eleven spokesmen gave reply for the opposition. The arguments were well-rehearsed; inconvenience to people served by the railway, the loss of this amenity to the Lake District National Park and the resulting effect on tourism, the implications for the CK&PR in the immediate and long-term future, the detrimental effect on Penrith, the limestone industry, the adverse effect on the economy, especially in the Vale of Eden. The disastrous effects which would result in additional road traffic on the A66 (there had been, in the previous two years, 440 accidents, 15 people killed, 92 maimed, 171 injured and 691 vehicles involved - and that could only get worse). Finally, the effects on the hotel industry were demonstrated (it was known that, during the previous season, 186 visitors had come to one hotel alone, who had travelled on the Eden Valley Railway; there must have been many more).

Mr K.B. Edwards, the barrister for the Appleby Borough, Penrith Urban and North Westmorland Rural Councils, pointed out that what the closure memorandum omitted to state was that, just as the travelling public were beginning to appreciate the line and make fuller use of the diesel trains, it was decided, after less than nine months, to cut back the services. Mr Edwards appeared to ruffle the inquiry chairman by speaking for a further 25 minutes, and was asked at that point either to finish within five minutes or, after the lunch break, to abbreviate the rest of his statement.

The barrister was not prepared to agree to this, pointing out that he was representing the groups most affected by the proposed closure. 'I have my instructions, and I am asked to present the full case. May I remind you, with respect, of the strictures which were meted out to Mr Justice Stable when he sought to hurry a jury!'

In continuing, he indicated that freight traffic over the Eden Valley Line during the last five months of the last year (1959), and on into 'this' year, had increased by 80 per cent, compared with a national figure of 12½ per cent to 15 per cent. 'This is a railway which has changed from being one of dubious payability into one of handsome payability.'

More objectors followed, and the hearing lasted four hours. It was clear that the opposition mounted against closure had been very considerable, and the case was a very strong one.

The hearing was followed by an hour's private deliberations, at the end of which the two area committees made a statement by way of recommendation to the Central Transport Consultative Committee (CTCC) in London:

1. That the complete closure of the line should be postponed and reconsidered in 18 months' time. For that period, a diesel passenger and parcels service should be continued while maximum economies are made by all possible means, including diversion of freight and mineral traffic to alternative routes, in the belief that this should effect substantial economies.
2. They urge that, for the next two summer seasons, the railways should increase their effort to attract more tourist traffic to this line.

The objectors saw this as a minor triumph, in spite of the decision to divert traffic. Talk of a reprieve was rife, and there was a feeling that British Railways was bowing to the enormous weight of opinion against closure.

Further, for the first time, the Press had been allowed proper access to most of the hearing. Freedom of information could only help the cause.

One of the first warning notes that all was not well was sounded on Tuesday 5th July, when Alderman J.R.S. Middlewood, a former station master and goods agent, reported to the Bishop Auckland Urban Council that in his view the BTC was not honouring the promise to consider for 18 months the proposal to close the east-west link. Mineral traffic had almost ceased on the line. The council decided to protest to the BTC.

By December the whole issue was open again, and the groups fighting closure discovered that once more they had to defend their corner, as they had done in February. In fact, there was a virtual re-run of the hearing of that date. The consultative committee in London was not impressed, it seems, with the outcome on that occasion.

It was claimed by the chairman, Sir Patrick Hamilton, at the meeting convened on 9th December (1960) for a joint gathering of the TUCC for the NW and NE, that the main purpose was to review the decision to divert freight traffic from the line and also consider whether the withdrawal of passenger services was sensible. The meeting was held in Newcastle, one step (albeit quite a large one) further away from the previous meeting in Carlisle. It meant the objectors had to make an even greater effort to be present - but present they were.

The meeting covered much of the ground covered in February. British Railways now argued that the withdrawal of passenger services would save £30,000 each year. The objectors argued that, if freight traffic was fully restored and greater publicity was given to the passenger services, the line had a realistic future. It was also suggested that a Government subsidy to enable rural areas to 'keep alive' was merited in this case.

Once again, for four hours, the two sides slogged it out. Mr A.M. Fell, representing Kirkby Stephen Chamber of Trade, put in a powerful plea for the retention of the line. 'I do feel,' he commented, 'that the Transport Commission, in proposing to close the Eden Valley Line, are wanting to take the cream of the traffic but are not prepared to put up with the inconveniences of the less remunerative local services. In other words, they want to have their cake and eat it.'

Mr G.N.C. Swift, Clerk of the Cumberland County Council, was equally vigorous. He reminded the meeting, once again, that the Eden Valley Line was not a small branch line . . . 'It is a link connecting two large sections of the country, East and West . . .'

He then went on to criticise those in authority for not having a proper national policy, which would have to take account of rural areas and places such as Penrith and Kirkby Stephen. 'Our problems as a whole in this country are not being dealt with at a high level in a sensible and intelligent fashion; there is nobody looking over the whole thing. It is like the film "The Wizard of Oz" - when you get to the top, there isn't one!'

Numerous other speakers listed argument after argument, although nothing new seemed to emerge. The recently rehearsed arguments had already been exhaustive.

At the end of the meeting, Mr Watson Sayer questioned the British Railways' figures, on which the closure plans were essentially based. He understood the railway was losing £700 each week. 'Did it really cost £190 each day, to run three trains each way between Penrith and Barnard Castle?'

Further, he felt the figures were unrealistic because they were 18 months out of date, and the situation had improved over that period. A strong appeal was made that a decision should be deferred pending a ruling by the Government about the subsidising of certain unremunerative lines.

After a review of the evidence, the TUCCs were divided in their view.

In January, the NW decided to support closure, but was not supported in this by the NE. Perhaps this was the sort of split British Railways had hoped for, weakening, as it could well do, the power of the opposition. As a result, the proposals were referred back for further consideration.

On Thursday 8th June, 1961, the groups fighting for the retention of the line suffered a serious set-back. At a meeting in Darlington, the North Eastern Area Transport Users' Committee decided to come down on the side of withdrawing passenger services and closing the sections of line as proposed by British Railways.

It was clear that a crisis was now approaching. This was highlighted by people such as Mr A.G. Braithwaite of Kirkby Stephen who wrote the following as part of a letter to the *Cumberland and Westmorland Herald*, which appeared on 1st July, 1961:

As I understand the question of the proposed closure of the (EVR) line is to be raised in Parliament on Monday 3rd July, may I . . . ask your readers who favour its retention to make one more effort to keep it open . . . Time is now against us and if we are to help we must do it NOW - not tomorrow or next week but TODAY . . . Write at once to either Mr Boyden or our own Member of Parliament, Mr Vane, or to any other of the MPs . . . and demand that a whole-hearted all-out fight be made in order to leave the Government and Minister of Transport in no doubt that we are prepared to fight to the bitter end . . .

In the same edition, BR London Midland Region advertised trips by train. These included weekday trips to Darlington:

Depart				
	Penrith	10.55	10s.	3d.
	Appleby East	11.20	8s.	3d.
	Warcop	11.27	7s.	0d.
	Kirkby Stephen East	11.38	6s.	3d.

Return from Darlington 4.34 pm

It seemed very much business as usual.

However, with the North Western Area and North Eastern Areas now in agreement, there seemed little hope for the opponents; it was assumed the CTCC would accept the case for closure.

Sure enough, at a meeting on Tuesday, 11th July, the CTCC did just that. All that was needed was confirmation by the Minister of Transport, Ernest Marples.

In a statement after the meeting, Sir Ronald Garrett, chairman of the committee, commented: 'We shall draw the attention of the Minister to the extreme local feeling which has been aroused over the matter. We will also draw attention to the fact that this is not a branch line and that a lot of other lines which feed into it might be affected by the closure.'

That night, a strong protest against the proposal to close the line was tabled in a Parliamentary motion. This was signed by ten MPs with constituencies in the North East, and included Mr James Boyden (Bishop Auckland) and Mr Chuter Ede (South Shields).

The motion was worded as follows:

This House views with concern the threatened closure of the Barnard Castle to Penrith railway line, the possibility of more branch line closures resulting therefrom, the damage which will be caused to the economy of Durham, the North Riding, Cumberland and Westmorland, the hardship which will be inflicted on the rural and mining communities of Teesdale and the Eden Valley and the loss of an amenity to the urban population of Tees-side and Durham, and urges the Minister of Transport to direct the British Transport Commission to maintain this through route and improve its efficiency.

In an editorial in the *Cumberland and Westmorland Herald* on Saturday 15th July, 1961, following this meeting, the writer expresses very plainly what many must have been feeling about the way in which events were developing:

Nobody can complain that the future of the Eden Valley line has not been debated with the utmost thoroughness at both area and national levels. What we can complain about is that these last two years have been marked by vacillation and indecision, recommendations and rejections.

(The writer later points out that) British Railways have shown a lamentable lack of any real attempt to give this line a chance to survive. From the first they have given the impression of being determined to get rid of it.

During the deliberations involving the fight against closure, a number of individuals emerged, who did much to try and prevent the closure of the line. One in particular, referred to earlier, was Mr Watson Sayer of Kirkby Stephen. Mr Sayer had a vested interest in that he owned limestone quarries near Brough, and relied heavily on the EVR for the transportation of this commodity from Warcop, where a special loading point had been made.

He attended numerous meetings, both public and private, in an attempt to convince the various groups involved that, with the right approach, the line could be run at a profit. So convinced was Mr Sayer about this that he eventually offered either to buy or rent the line, which he felt could be made a going concern. Perhaps the biggest indictment against British Railways concerning its motives for the future of this line was in the refusal to consider either of these proposals. Mr Sayer was turned down. The day of privatisation had not yet dawned!

On Thursday 7th December, 1961, almost a year after the second major hearing, Mr Boyden MP received a letter from the Minister of Transport, Mr Ernest Marples. It informed him that a decision had been made to close the EVR. No date was given for the closure. Mr Marples pointed out that he had accepted the recommendation of the Consultative Committee and this decision was being passed on to the BTC.

Mr Boyden was moved to comment: 'This is turning down as wide a body of protest as the Minister must have had over any closure.'

It says much for the sheer tenacity of the groups opposing the closure that they did not see this as the end of the fight.

Although it was eventually announced that the last train would run on Saturday 20th January, 1962, a group met at Barnard Castle on Friday 5th January, in an attempt to make a last ditch stand.

The meeting consisted of representatives from a number of Borough Councils. Mr Boyden presided and among those present was Mr Watson Sayer.

After a long discussion, in which the arguments against closure were yet again carefully rehearsed, additional points were made. It was alleged that errors and misleading omissions had been made in the evidence given by the BTC to the Minister of Transport; that the method of conduct of the inquiry at Newcastle gave no opportunity to objectors to question the Commission's witnesses; that the railway had been badly mismanaged; that there were unknown quantities of coal, copper, lead and silver in the Pennines, which might be worked in future.

At the end of the lengthy meeting it was unanimously decided to ask the Minister to receive a deputation, and a case was prepared in readiness.

In a reply to the Clerk of Barnard Castle Rural District Council, Mr Marples declined to meet the group to discuss matters further. The Minister felt that all that needed to be said had been said. That was the end of the matter.

After some two years of dedicated fighting, of which Russell Elliot and his colleagues would no doubt have been justifiably proud, the battle was lost.

Closure date stood at 20th January, 1962.

The event was an emotional one for many who witnessed it. All the various formalities which, sadly, became commonplace over the next few years on a considerable number of branch lines, were observed.

The last scheduled train was from Penrith to Darlington. A civic send-off was arranged and large numbers of people joined the train. A rake of four coaches was used to convey them. A party of about 100 others formed, to give the train a proper send-off, gathering at the EVR 'bay' of the station.

Just after 8.30 pm, Mr T.K. Jones, chairman of the Penrith Urban Council, who also bought the very last ticket (Penrith to Clifton Moor), but chose to give it to an enthusiast, blew the whistle, and the train left. A lamp bearing the insignia of the S&D was also used in the ceremony.

At Appleby, a much larger crowd had gathered, and the station was packed with people. The mayor, Alderman J.F. Whitehead, was present, together with the Town Clerk, Mr H.A. Jones. The Appleby Town Band, under the direction of Mr F.S. Potts, gave a musical contribution to the event by playing 'Auld Lang Syne'.

A wreath was placed on the front of the diesel locomotive by Mr F.J. Eggleston for the Chamber of Trade. It bore the inscription 'In memory of 100 years of faithful service, R.I.P.'

By the time the train reached Kirkby Stephen, it is reckoned that between 500 and 600 people had gathered at the station. A group of four, Mr J. Hunt, Mr Tom Potter, Mr Watson Sayer and Mr Ivan Hodgson had equipped themselves with ancient cycles - a final protest, with a number of slogans, displaying their views: 'Back 100 Years'.

Kirkby Stephen Silver Band played and, at 9.15 pm, the train set out for Barnard Castle and Darlington. The EVR had seen its last scheduled passenger train.

Following close behind the diesel came an enthusiasts' special, 'The Stainmore Limited'. The train, organised by the Railway Correspondence and Travel Society, was hauled by BR Standard class '3MT' 2-6-0 No. 77003 and Standard class '4MT' 2-6-0 No. 76049.

Reflecting on the event, as the Special left for Stainmore, one local reporter wrote: 'Soon, it too was gone and with it went an era in the social history not only of Kirkby Stephen but the whole Eden Valley.'

A forlorn looking Kirkby Stephen East seen looking west on 19th April, 1971. Only the single track from Appleby to Hartley Quarry remains.   *C.A. Allenby*

Chapter Twelve

The Aftermath

British Railways had been accused of promise-breaking during the long-drawn-out process of deciding the future (or, in the event, the lack of it) for the line. However, once the objective had been realised, and the line was closed, one promise, that of removing the track, was achieved with remarkable speed. Some have speculated that the Board were anxious to avoid any back-lash which might have brought renewed pressure on them for the line to be used in some way, or possibly to prevent visits by enthusiasts' specials. Whatever the reason or reasons, tracklifting began later in 1962.

By the end of the year, the only remaining sections of the valley line left were at the westerly end, where the section from the Eden Valley Junction to Clifton Moor was retained for freight, and the easterly section from Appleby to the Hartley Quarries.

Clifton Moor retained its freight facility until 6th July, 1964, whereas the quarry traffic continued a further 10 years until the end of October 1974. Once the quarry traffic ceased, the track beyond Flitholme, just to the west of Warcop, was also removed.

The section between Appleby and Warcop continued to be used, as it provided a facility for the army training area at Warcop. On at least one occasion, a train standing in Warcop station was attacked by the SAS - but only in the course of training!

Freight was carried until March 1989, and on a number of occasions enthusiasts' specials visited this section of the branch, travelling down to Warcop, the last of these being in 1990. These various trains had classes '31', '40' and '47' as their motive power.

In 1993, the points at the east end of Warcop station were removed and taken to British Gypsum at Kirkby Thore (Midland). This move made it impossible to run a locomotive round its train at Warcop.

Speculation about the future use of this section continued. There are those of the opinion that live ammunition, being brought into Warcop, should be carried by rail and not by road. BR was coy about making any statements, although they were not willing to sell sections of the trackbed to local people who made an approach, maintaining that the MOD had not determined its contract to use the line. However, in 1995 there was a significant development.

In the meantime, during 1993, a track-testing machine was taken along the section, but it appears it was twice derailed, such was the poor state of the track.

During 1989, test drilling had been carried out in the goods yard at Warcop by a firm hoping to extract water for bottling. The first drilling was satisfactory, but another, only a few yards away, proved less so, and the project appears to have been abandoned.

The recession of the 1980s devastated the industries both of the North-East and North-West, and the 'link' so keenly fought for in the late 1950s and early 1960s would probably no longer be justified. Millions of pounds have been and

English Electric type '4' class '40' No. 40 086 carrying 'The Whistler' headboard is seen at Appleby as it returns from Warcop, 6th October, 1984. *Tom Heavyside*

Class '47' No. 47 617 heads a train of condemned coaches heading for MOD Warcop for use in a training exercise (*see page 103*), 9th April, 1987. *N.E. Stead*

A Hunslet-Barclay weedkiller train approaches Warcop in July 1989. The building on the right, almost completely overgrown, is the signal box. *N.E. Stead*

Hunslet-Barclay class '20' No. 20 902 passes Warcop goods yard with a weedkiller train on 17th July, 1989. *N.E. Stead*

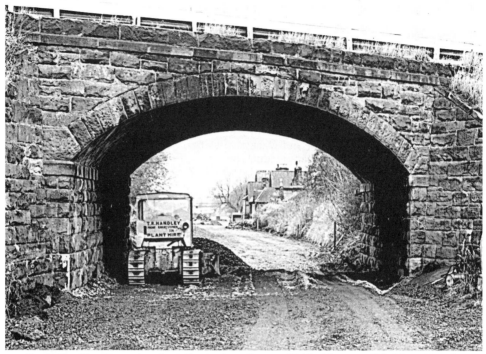

Overbridge No. 67 carrying the A68 over the railway at Kirkby Thore on 12th July, 1972. The station was demolished during a road improvement scheme in the 1980s. The goods yard was to the right, behind the photographer. *P. Singlehurst*

Temple Sowerby station buildings, 17th April, 1970. *P. Singlehurst*

are being spent in improving the A66 over Stainmore, and much of it is now dual carriageway. Whilst it might be argued that a fraction of this amount would have kept the railway open, the goods being carried by heavy lorries are very diverse and go to a wide variety of destinations. It is difficult to imagine that these loads would ever have been taken by rail.

As far as the buildings are concerned, with the exception of Kirkby Thore, all the stations on the EVR are now private dwellings and so have a future. (It is interesting to note that the old Musgrave station has been renamed 'Beech Ings'!) Skygarth and Musgrave viaducts have long gone, although the piers can still be seen. Coupland Beck viaduct is still intact, as it is in the section where the track has not been removed. A great deal of the old track bed can still be clearly seen, as can road bridges, underpasses and some lineside buildings.

A journey up the Vale of Eden from Kirkby Stephen to Penrith is a pleasant one and for the student of railway archaeology has its rewards. The only regret, especially on a sunny summer evening, is that it is a journey that can no longer be made by train.

Recent developments, however, suggest that this may once again be possible, at least in part . . .

Plans to Restore and Re-open the Line, 1995-1996

As mentioned earlier, the section of track between Appleby and Warcop had remained intact, following the closure of the rest of the line.

In the early part of 1995, British Rail announced the intention to sell this section, the MOD having decided it had no further use for it. Although overgrown and showing signs of dilapidation, this section is certainly not beyond restoration.

David Birmingham, a man with an interest in the line, was very much aware of this, and has decided to try and raise £1m. to put this part of the line back in working order. The important links with the Settle and Carlisle at Appleby would be a vital element in turning the EVR into a tourist attraction.

There has been considerable local support for the scheme and on 28th September, 1995 the inaugural meeting of the Eden Valley Railway Society (EVRS) was held. At this meeting, proposals for re-opening the line were discussed and a committee was formed. This consists of David Birmingham (Chairman), Michael Froud (Vice Chairman and Civil Engineer), John Birmingham (Vice Chairman), David Adams (Secretary and Treasurer), David Greenhalgh (Membership Secretary), Robert Western (Press Officer), Richard Holden, Paul Ladhams, Ian March, Michael Owen, Robert Scott and Brian White.

At the first meeting of this committee it was agreed that whilst the re-opening of the section of line from Appleby to Warcop is the priority, there should be further phases which include the sections from Warcop to Kirkby Stephen and beyond Kirkby Stephen, eastwards, to Stainmore Summit, with the possible rebuilding of the famous Belah viaduct.

On 28th November a meeting was held with a representative of the British

The signal box at Cliburn still stands - although it is only a shell. The owner is seen giving it a coat of paint - helping to preserve it for posterity! The station is on the right. *Author*

Warcop station, now a private dwelling. The track is still in place here and remains so all the way to Appleby. *Author*

Rail Property Board with a view to purchasing the line from Appleby to Warcop and discussions are still taking place to that end.

A survey of the line has been carried out and the cost of reinstating that section has been determined.

At present the whole project has three phases.

The first is to reopen the line where track still exists and together with this to rebuild Belah viaduct as a monument to the men who were the inspiration and operators of the railways in the North-East.

This scheme is tied in with the celebration of the millenium and millenium funding is being sought.

The second phase involves the re-opening of the line from Warcop to Kirkby Stephen with the possible use of the old Kirkby Stephen station and site as a visitor centre.

The final and very ambitious section is to reinstate the railway from Kirkby Stephen on to Stainmore and so use the (rebuilt) Belah viaduct. It is reckoned the last phase will not be completed before the year 2010.

In the meantime, membership of the Eden Valley Railway Society continues to grow and plans for the scheme have been met with enthusiasm both locally and nationally. (Details of how to apply for membership are given in Appendix Two.)

Further, the Eden Valley Railway trust has been established and also the Eden Valley Railway Company formed.

A boost was given to the scheme in 1996 when Viscount Whitelaw agreed to become the President of the Society.

It seems that as each day passes the plans to bring steam back to the Eden Valley Railway become more and more of a reality.

Who knows, perhaps Russell Elliot is having a quiet chuckle somewhere . . .

The station building at Temple Sowerby is now a fine private dwelling.   *Author*

Some Significant Dates in
the History of the EVR

1857	(December)	Prospectus issued.
1858	(May)	Act (Vict. Reg. 21 Cap. xiv) for building the line.
	(August)	Cutting of the first sod by Lord Brougham.
1861	(October)	Directors travel the length of the line.
1862	(April)	Goods traffic commences.
	(June)	Opens to passengers. S&D takes over EVR.
	(July)	Act (Vict. Reg. 25 & 26 Cap. cxviii) for the Northern curve.
1863	(August)	Northern Curve opens. NER takes over the S&D, and hence the EVR.
1864	(June)	Act (Vict. Reg. 27 & 28 Cap. lxvii) for a line from Eamont Junction to Red Hills.
1866	(September)	Red Hills spur opens.
1874	(July)	Act (Vict. Reg. 37 & 38 Cap. cxxxiv) to abandon Southern curve.
1880-1893		Trains run from Appleby to Penrith in conjunction with MR.
1952	(November)	Musgrave station closed completely.
1953	(December)	Kirkby Thore station closed completely. Temple Sowerby closed to passengers; goods facilities retained.
1956	(September)	Cliburn closed completely.
1958	(February)	'Faster' diesel service introduced; Penrith to Darlington.
1959	(December)	Proposal to withdraw passenger services and close sections of the line.
1960	(February)	Petitions made to retain line (meeting of the NW & NE TUCC in Carlisle).
	(December)	Further meeting at Newcastle.
1961	(July)	CTCC announce intention to close, subject to confirmation by Minister of Transport.
	(December)	Ernest Marples confirms closure.
1962	(January)	Last train (20.1.62). Line closes with the exception of a section from Appleby to Warcop and the western end.
1964	(July)	Goods facility to Clifton Moor ceases.
1974	(October)	Quarry traffic ceases. Track removed beyond Flitholme.

The section from Appleby to Warcop was used from time to time until into the 1980s.

1993		Run-round facility at Warcop removed.

Appendix Two

The Eden Valley Railway Company Preservation Society

The Society has been formed to support a scheme to re-open the old EVR between Appleby and Warcop, and to explore the possibility of extending the line eastwards to Kirkby Stephen and then Stainmore Summit.

A quarterly newsletter is issued, to keep members in touch and enable them to contribute and make their views known. There is the opportunity for regular meetings.

Annual membership £10; Life Membership is £150. Details can be obtained from the Membership Secretary:

David Greenhalgh,
Hillcroft,
Colby,
Appleby,
Cumbria, CA16 6BD.

Telephone: 01768-352822.

Author's Note

The correct spelling of 'Elliot' almost remains something of a mystery. The Admiral actually appears to be inconsistent himself! His letters are signed 'Elliot' and yet when signing the Board Minutes, he signs 'Eliott' (unless someone is signing incorrectly - on his behalf). The gravestones carry the spelling 'Eliott' (would he have accepted an error in such circumstances?) and O'Byrne's Naval Biography uses 'Eliott'. The spelling 'Elliott' often found in Press reports can certainly be discounted. This account uses the spelling found at the bottom of the letters, namely 'Elliot'. The author has been unable to find a photograph of Admiral Elliot, in spite of an intensive search. If any reader knows the wherabouts of such a photograph, the author would be pleased to hear about it.

Thanks

I am especially grateful to Michael Wild of Natland, Cumbria, who used his word-processor to turn my handwritten account into a legible text for the publisher. My thanks also, to the Staffs of the various libraries and archive departments, mentioned in the list of 'Locations', for being so helpful; also to the people who responded to my requests for information, and to a number of people who provided contemporary accounts of the line, especially Mr Arthur Watson of Brough, a former fireman, whose anecdotes (not all included!) and information are very much appreciated.

Sources

Russell Elliot's letters
Extracts from the Minutes of Shareholders' Meetings of the following companies:
Eden Valley Railway
South Durham & Lancashire Union Railway
Stockton & Darlington Railway
Cockermouth, Keswick and Penrith Railway
North Eastern Railway

Various Bills with plans deposited for presentation to Parliament and copies of the Acts for various schemes.

The Cumberland & Westmorland Herald
The Westmorland Gazette
The Kendal Mercury
The Illustrated Times
Naval Biography by O'Byrne
Milner's Guides to Railways, Coaches and Steamers in the North of England
Timetables - various
Clinker's Register of Closed Passenger Stations and Goods Depots in England, Scotland and Wales 1830-1980 by C.R. Clinker, Avon-Anglia
An Illustrated History of NER Locomotives by Ken Hoole, Oxford Publishing Co.
Locomotives of the LNER, RCTS
Locomotives of the North Eastern Railway by O.S. Nock, Ian Allan
North Eastern Locomotive Sheds by Ken Hoole, David & Charles
The North Eastern Railway by C.J. Allen, Ian Allan
Westmorland Church Notes (1889). In 2 volumes, by E. Belassis
Local knowledge

Locations

Cumbria Record Office (Kendal)
Kendal Library
Penrith Library
House of Lords Library
Darlington Railway Museum and Ken Hoole Study Centre
National Maritime Museum (Information Centre), Greenwich
Royal Naval Museum (Information Centre), Portsmouth
The Public Record Office, Kew

Brunel University Transport Collection prints are available from W.R. Burton, 3 Fairway, Clifton, York, YO3 6QA.